Frontispiece (next page): A kendo practice session in full swing at the famous Mitsubishi Company's kendo hall in their Tokyo main-office building.

THIS IS Kendo

The Art of Japanese Fencing

by Junzo Sasamori
and Gordon Warner

Charles E. Tuttle Company: Publishers
RUTLAND, VERMONT & TOKYO, JAPAN

Representatives
For Continental Europe:
BOXERBOOKS, INC., Zurich
For the British Isles:
PRENTICE-HALL INTERNATIONAL, INC., London
For Australasia:
BOOK WISE (AUSTRALIA) PTY. LTD.
104–108 Sussex Street, Sydney 2000

Published by the Charles E. Tuttle Company, Inc.
of Rutland, Vermont & Tokyo, Japan
with editorial offices at
Suido 1-chome, 2-6, Bunkyo-ku, Tokyo

Copyright in Japan, 1964
by Charles E. Tuttle Company

Library of Congress Catalog
Card No. 64-22900

International Standard Book No. 0-8048-0574-1

First printing, 1964
Fifteenth printing, 1984

Layout of illustrations by S. Katakura
PRINTED IN JAPAN

絶妙剣

笹森順造

[on previous page]
Calligraphy by Junzo Sasamori:
Zetsumyo-ken, the sword miraculous,
with signature and seals.

Table of Contents

Contents

List of Illustrations

13

Foreword

As president of the Japan Amateur Athletic Association, I have followed with great interest the development by Dr. Gordon Warner and Dr. Junzo Sasamori, the two authors of the manuscript *This Is Kendo,* which introduces the Japanese art of kendo. It is the first book ever written on kendo in a language other than Japanese.

As a Japanese, I have an intense feeling of satisfaction in the extensive background of the two authors, their devotion to perfection, scholarly approach, and knowledge of the martial arts of Japan. To undertake the task of writing on a Japanese art is difficult enough, and more so when the subject is a profound ancient art. Kendo, the Japanese art of fencing, has a long cultural history interwoven in the very fiber of the Japanese people themselves.

There has long been a need for this text on the bookshelves of Western nations. Therefore it is with a deep sense of pride that I personally and officially endorse this publication as a book that can be read for a true and sincere understanding of the art of kendo, a facet of our Japanese culture.

JUICHI TSUSHIMA
Member of the House of Councillors,
National Diet, and
President,
Japan Amateur Athletic Association

Introduction

This book introduces kendo, the exhilarating mental and physical sport of Japan that has gained new popularity, with both sexes now participating. Kendo was originally the Japanese feudal art of swordsmanship. Through its own evolution and the efforts of a remarkable group of teachers it has progressed through the years to its present position as a sport. Its theory, techniques, and methods of training, developed by the various schools, have been handed down through the centuries and today have been moulded into an educative sport with all of the action and history of the past con‑ tained within its present training. Kendo could easily find its place among the events of the Olympic Games, since most of the Olympic events have been developed from the arts of fighting or hunting.

Today in Japan the sport of kendo is a part of the regular curriculum in the educational system from the secondary-school level to the university. The student participating in kendo has the unique opportunity of studying firsthand an activity that has followed the continuous growth of his country from the historical past to the present. Followers of the sport find that it is not only a way of preparing for life during youth but also a code that can be carried on throughout all of life.

The love and pleasure of kendo practice among the Japanese does not end with graduation from school. Kendo teams or fencing clubs can be found in almost every city of Japan. Large companies have their own fenc- ing halls, as do the state and municipal public service departments, which encourage participation and organize teams. Each year the All-Japan Stu- dent Kendo Federation draws increasing numbers of contestants and

17

spectators. The All-Japan Kendo Federation Match Championships, which are held in the great Meiji Sports Palace in Tokyo, offer the Emperor's Cup as an award to the grand champion. The deep attachment to kendo by those who follow the sport is clearly indicated by the fact that today there are kendoists over seventy and even over eighty years of age who take part in matches, and many undergo graded promotional examinations every year. One kendoist who has reached ninety still participates in matches.

The motivation behind this sport is its tremendous historical significance. Japanese children today listen with gaping mouths at the storyteller's booth to tales of the samurai, and they leave with their heads spinning with the adventures of Yoshitsune and his faithful retainer Benkei or of the two Soga brothers. At home, older brother is pleaded with to read the life of Miyamoto Musashi, the famous 17th-century samurai who wielded two swords.

The Japanese knight had a counterpart, although the two were unknown to each other. The European knight flourished in the midst of intrigue and conspiracy, as did the samurai. A comparison of their ethics and ideals reveals some points of difference in codes and proprieties, but these differences are only slight. The love for the sport of kendo is the realization that one is participating in an art developed by the samurai during those years when knighthood in Japan meant the same as knighthood in Europe. Valor, honesty, integrity, and patience formed the basis for developing a code of ethical rules for the samurai, and such rules are taught to the youth of today so that they will have an understanding of the value of worthwhile living for the world of tomorrow. Generally those who practice kendo from the very beginning in their youth are found to be courteous, healthy, dependable, good in academic fields, and pleasing in personality. These are the true traits of the noble samurai as handed down to the youth of today for their conduct of life.

It is important also to remember that less than eighty years ago Bushido (the way of the *bushi* or samurai) was followed in daily life in Japan. The polite formality in the home, as well as the strict adherence to custom on the street, the rules of the sword and the road, all leisure salutations and the politest forms of speech in stately places, the canons of art and conduct, as well as of service to daimyo or shogun—these formed the universal creed of the Japanese in the castled city and in the province. In these, as a living school of thought and life, boy and girl alike were trained.

Notably, the samurai were men of action. Their life smacked of the life of America's western frontier in the roaring mid-1800's. Among the favorite samurai maxims was "To know and to act, one and the same." Through kendo, which is the modern sport adapted from this most intriguing past, the beginner will learn that the final stress is laid on the basic substance of its inspiration: hard work, understanding, training, respect for elders, and —above all—patience.

This book, which actually had its beginning twenty-five years ago, springs from the belief that there is a need for a systematic overview of the Japanese martial arts, which in the context of the contemporary world are sports. The art of kendo has emerged certainly not because of its pure physical power but because of its deep mental training and its philosophical outlook on everyday living.

The presentation of the historical development of a martial art in a culture is an overwhelming task. In this volume we have wanted to serve two functions which are inseparably linked but which are all too frequently regarded as distinct. The book attempts in the first place to offer a survey of the Japanese art of kendo that will be of service to the student contemplating a study of the knighthood and Bushido of feudal Japan. In the second place the book is directed toward the person who is not anticipating a study of the sport of kendo itself but who desires a text that will add enlightenment to his interest and support him in his desire to better understand the culture of Japan. Attention has also been given to details of interest to the beginner as well as to the veteran kendoist.

The development of the historical and philosophical facets of kendo and of the psychological methods employed in the training can be understood by the kendoist today, just as they were understood by his counterpart in feudal Japan who trained to become a samurai. The paramount point to be remembered in this book on an ancient art is that no one really stops learning more about the people who invented armor and developed combat techniques. It is our hope that the reader will continue his study beyond the scope of this book.

We welcome you to study our small volume and hope that in doing so

19

Introduction

you will be touched by the deep philosophy behind the mask and that you will understand the culture of Japan and work with the younger generation to cultivate international good will.

It would be unfitting for us to close this introduction without expressing our gratitude to all of our friends who have helped to make this book possible—particularly to such outstanding kendoists as Moriji Mochida, Sennosuke Masuda, Toshiro Watanabe, and Ko Noda. To others in the long list of inspiring kendoists, our deep thanks for their support. We are grateful also to the Mitsubishi Dojo, the Hosei University Kendo Team, the Tobukan in Mito, the Myogi Dojo, and others for the use of their facilities. We have been encouraged by the full approval and sanction of the All-Japan Kendo Federation, the All-Japan Student Kendo Federation, and the American Kendo Federation in our project. We are equally indebted to Mr. Kenji Miyamura, head of the Mainichi Newspaper Haneda Press Bureau, and to Mr. Tanaka, of the Pan-Asia Newspaper Bureau, for the excellent photographs that illustrate the book. Finally, we wish to express our appreciation to the Charles E. Tuttle Company for its encouragement in our undertaking of this publishing venture.

JUNZO SASAMORI
GORDON WARNER

THIS IS KENDO

問字は一時の恥
問わぬは末代の恥

Tou wa ichiji no haji,
towanu wa matsudai no haji
To ask may be a moment's shame, but not to ask
and remain ignorant is a lifelong shame

1

The Kendo Tradition

Beginnings

It is stated in the opening paragraph of the Japanese government's publication, *Japan: Its Land, People, and Culture,* that the "exact date when the ancestors of the [Yamato] people first settled in the Japanese islands and developed their own culture...remains shrouded in obscurity." Thus it is apparent that little factual knowledge remains of Japan's ancient past.

In the two great anthologies, the *Kojiki* and the *Nihon-shoki,* dating from the early 8th century A.D., are brought together a large number of the old Japanese legends, and in the writings of later periods the great wealth of historical landmarks in the life of the Japanese people are ready for the researcher. These old legends make up part of the Japanese national history, and as each nation has its own particular legendary character, each national story is cherished by the population with a personal pride.

In the study of Japan's historical past, as in the study of any Asian country's past, there will be found specific periods and eras, with the name of each era corresponding to that of the ruling head, but seldom can one find a Christian calendar date to pinpoint the ancient Japanese event in a given Western period of history. For the general orientation of the reader as he follows the history of kendo in this opening chapter, an outline of Japanese historical periods is given below. With this ready reference chart at hand, he can place events in Japanese history correspondently in his own Western historical background.

At this point a note on Japanese personal and era names is pertinent. It must be remembered that in Japan, as in China and Korea, the family name precedes the given name, although in this book, except for the names of feudal daimyo, the Western practice of given name first is followed. It was not until after the Meiji Restoration of 1867 that all Japanese families came to have family names. During the Tokugawa period (1600–1867), just prior to the Meiji Restoration, only the people of the court or the military classes used family names. It should be further pointed out that in Japan even the Imperial Family does not have a name of its own. Therefore only the era name is listed, and when the present emperor came to the throne in 1926 he was known as Michi no Miya Hirohito, although his name will be placed in history as that of Showa (1926–   ). For the convenience of the reader, era names appearing in the text are identified in terms of Western-style dates.

Prehistoric times	
Non-pottery culture	(date unknown)
Jomon-shiki culture	before 300 B.C.
Yayoi-shiki culture	before 200 B.C.
Ancient times	
Early ancient times	
Period of tribal states	A.D. 57 to 6th century
Yamato period	6th century to 645
Later ancient times	
Period of adoption from the Chinese	645 to 784
Taika Reform period	645 to 710
Nara period	710 to 784
Heian period	784 to 1184
Fujiwara period	866 to 1160
Taira period	1160 to 1184
Medieval times (early feudal times)	
Kamakura period	1184 to 1333
Period of Minamoto rule	1184 to 1199
Transition period: Minamoto to Hojo rule	1199 to 1219
Period of Hojo rule	1219 to 1333
Period of Kemmu Restoration	1334 to 1336
Ashikaga (Muromachi) period	1336 to 1568
Azuchi-Momoyama period	1568 to 1600
Early modern times (later feudal times)	

Tokugawa (Edo) period	1600 to 1868
Modern times	
Meiji era	1868 to 1912
Taisho era	1912 to 1926
Showa era	1926 to present

Generally a country will have throughout the periods of every century of its own history many chapters written on its particular martial arts. Also, a country will have a national martial art or arts particular to its own culture. The archives of some national libraries hold exciting literature for anyone who cares to hold an armchair conference covering such interesting martial facets of a respective country.

There remains a wealth of such material hidden in the Chinese ideograms of ancient Japanese writings that tell of the struggle for existence by the Japanese *bushi* and later the knights or samurai. The most important fact about the history of kendo, although this martial art was not called that in the beginning, is that it developed out of Japan's long historical past and is entirely an original art with the Japanese.

It is difficult for even the most able scholars to produce accurately dated historical studies from the three volumes of the *Kojiki*. The material deals with the period from the mythological ages down to the reign of Suiko Tenno (Empress Suiko, 592–628). The same problem is met in working with the thirty volumes of the *Nihon-shoki,* completed in 720. These volumes follow the history of Japan from the mythological ages down to the reign of Jito Tenno (Empress Jito, 686–97).

These two documents are generally utilized by Japanese historians to cover the many facets of the ancient past, and it is in them that the first reference is made to Choisai Iizasa in connection with the founding of *kenjutsu* (*ken* means sword and *jutsu* technique or art, and together they mean swordsmanship).

Other historians select Kunimatsu no Mahito as the founder of this ancient art because he was the direct descendant of Amatsu Koyane no Mikoto and was famous as a swordsman. This fable continues with the idea that Kunimatsu no Mahito's style of swordsmanship was the *Kashima no tachi* or Kashima Shrine style of the sword. The Japanese are aware that

25

Mahito is not a real name, but they have called the style or form of such swordsmanship by this name, and it has continued to be so called through the centuries down to the present.

Early Japanese historians claimed that there were three stages or periods in the ancient history of swordsmanship: the *joko-ryu* (ancient style), the *chuko-ryu* (middle style), and the *shinto-ryu* (new style). These three stages made up the development of Kunimatsu no Mahito's style, which is considered as the beginning of the sword techniques of the early Japanese warriors. However, it is necessary to realize that there was no organized, definite form or style of sword fighting at this time.

Development of an art

During the later years, about A.D. 400, there is found a reference to the use of the *bokken* as a weapon. The *bokken* style calls for the use of a solid wooden stick fashioned like a sword, keeping the shape, length, and weight as near those of a live blade as possible. The wood is extremely hard and is still used in Japan in modern times.

The wooden-sword technique was followed later by the art of *tachikaki*, or the form of drawing the sword from the *saya* or scabbard. At this time the *tachi* or *katana* blade of the long sword was straight, and the weapon was carried in a sling with the cutting edge of the blade turned downward toward the ground.

Although the Japanese warrior carried the long sword in a sling worn on the left side, it was not an invention peculiar to the Japanese. The Chinese had long carried a sword in this manner. However, the *bushi* (samurai) could draw their blade in a bold upward-sweeping movement from such a position. This "ground-to-sky" style, although not a standardized style of fighting, was generally carried out with rugged dispatch, and there is evidence that the opponent found its movement awesome in every degree.

Out of these various actions some dozens of different forms or styles called *ryu* were developed into techniques of fencing. As each fencing master improved his style of swordsmanship and it proved a factor in winning an

26

individual combat or turning the tide of battle, the fencing master would become famous for his particular style. The master swordsman would develop a specific style so that a warrior could practice, either with the long or the short sword, the many cuts, thrusts, and slashing movements used in battle. As the style proved successful, the master swordsman would give his own name to the particular fencing technique he had invented.

During the early Heian period much of Japanese culture was imported from China. There arose an overwhelming interest in things Chinese, and the people directed their attention away from the martial arts, devoting themselves primarily to philosophy, the arts, and the study of China's ancient culture. Such concentrated study kept the warrior away from the exercise halls of the martial arts, although some of the *bushi* were continuing their training in spite of the lack of general interest. This training was to be of great value, for in just a short span of years the *bushi* were called upon to assume an important role in the history of Japan.

There are seven main periods of later Japanese history, which begin with the Taika era (645–50) in the reign of the Emperor Kotoku. The first period extends over three hundred years (645–956) or from the first year of Taika, under Emperor Kotoku, to the tenth year of Tenryaku (947–56) during the reign of Emperor Murakami. With the reformation that took place during Taika, the conditions of the country underwent a great change. The people found that they were being organized under a uniform government. A system of prefectures was established and there was an inauguration of royal power in the form of a central government. The people also found that all the land was being placed entirely under state ownership. Local lords were appointed, and government officials were made to live within specific salaries granted by the imperial court.

The prefectural system continued until the amendment of the law under the Taiho Code of Emperor Mommu in 701, which was the first year of the Taiho era (701–3), and was subsequently amended by the Act of Engi under Emperor Daigo in 907.

It was during the rise of the *shoen* or manorial system that Yoshifusa Fujiwara (804–72) became the *sessho* (regent), making it the first time in Japanese history that a subject had risen to the position of regent. At the

27

same time in the Western world the word chivalry was being defined as that body of sentiment and practice, of law and custom, prevailing among the dominant European classes, beginning with the year 900.

From the Nara period (710–84), when the name *tachikaki* had given way to the new form of *tachiuchi* (match with swords), until the Muromachi period (1336–1568), there was a slow development in *kenjutsu* (use of the sword). It was the Muromachi period that re-established the popularity of *kenjutsu* and saw the beginning of the fencing schools called *dojo*. These schools were encouraged, and generally a *dojo* would have an exceptionally strong fencing master who would train the young *bushi* in *kenjutsu*.

Bushi and Bushido

Perhaps the most misused and misunderstood word in the English language is the term Bushido. Yet behind this term is one of the greatest moulding forces in the development of a national culture and education that the world has observed. This force was observed first in the way of life adopted by the Japanese samurai and later carried into daily living by the people.

A study of Bushido reveals much of the spirit of the nation itself. The statement that Bushido made Japan the energetic nation that it is today is quite true. There has been little real understanding of the term Bushido, however, since the Meiji edict of 1872 prohibiting the wearing of swords in public. That was the year of the Meiji proclamation instituting a new system of education and ending the long development of this prescribed way of life for so many—a way of life that had been tested and polished over many centuries and was deeply understood by all the people of the nation during this period. The samurai had made Bushido a living symbol of a way of life through their actions, and the stories of their lives made interesting reading.

The philosophy of Bushido as a force did not appear on the scene suddenly but arose as the total process of men wanting to live a life of service and in a regulated manner. Each step in this way of life was to be strictly laid down in clear terms for all to understand. The process of the development, the indigenous fashion of its rise, from the deep and widespread philosophical influences of the many facets of Japanese feudal society, can

28

1. The tradition of the Japanese samurai lives on in contemporary kendo. University kendo team at training session on the beach.

be carefully reviewed for an understanding of the people of modern Japan.

Briefly it is the task of this section of the book to open the door to a relatively obscure part of the culture of the Japanese people and to give some factual information on the principles, the philosophy, and the practice of Bushido in feudal Japan.

The term Bushido has often been spoken of as "the soul of old Japan." From the 13th century on, the samurai, or Japanese knights, came to play an increasingly important part in the political, social, and economic affairs of the young growing nation. Because of their part in the daily social living there was a need to develop a class self-consciousness; there was a need for a code of conduct for this class in their daily living and through this need a new force became a code.

A strong code of ethics was needed to draw these appallingly stern, ener-

getic, very idealistic, and sensitive individuals together as a force. It is further interesting to note that the code was not written down as simple rules of conduct or regulations, but it was strongly impressed in their minds through daily acts. The deep meaning of the code was brought into focus through the rigorous daily living practiced in feudal times.

This training of the mind and body was not just words but was accomplished through seemingly endless tasks; in every facet of life such was the training. It was the samurai's way of life, and he, as a man, was required to continue a course of daily training throughout his life to reach the goal of perfection.

Bushido, as a philosophy, had much in common with chivalry in the middle ages of Europe. However, Bushido had a great deal more that was distinctive and peculiar to itself. The high regard and position given the samurai by the people is one of the most important differences between feudal history in Japan, on the one hand, and China and Europe on the

30

2. Young kendoists of the Mito Tobukan, one of the chief centers of kendo today.

3. In spite of a period of decline after World War II kendo is again becoming popular with the youth. Elementary and High School enthusiasts during practice session.

4. The All-Japan Schoolteachers' Kendo Tournament (Osaka, 1962) is one of the main events of modern kendo.

5. Kendo is increasingly attracting international interest. A scene from the U.S.-Japan Kendo Tournament held in Kyoto in 1956.

other. In ancient China the soldier was as a rule despised, being placed at the very lowest rank of Chinese society. In later years, under the pressures and necessities of continuous continental strife, the Chinese soldier became quite respected. But in feudal Japan few were held more worthy of imitation than the *bushi,* later to become the samurai class. This has continued into present-day Japan.

Samurai ideals were taught in classes to the youth. Much of what is known of Bushido rises from fugitive verses. Love of beauty was expressed by way of poetry and was an essential part of the chivalrous code of the Japanese knight.

Significantly the samurai's most cherished possession was his sword. Yet, to use this weapon correctly took years of training, not so much in physical development alone, but in mental training as well. It was this philosophy of life that interested the population. The drama and poetry should be given the credit for keeping it constantly before society as a real part of the entire culture. Realism played a great part in the rise of Bushido, and the mental training in patience was as vital as was the physical skill in war with the sword.

This attitude of mental and physical training taken by the samurai towards the use of the sword became strongly ingrained in the very sinew of the Japanese people down to the modern period. Life was frugal and not easy for anyone, but the warmth of spiritual training was there.

Few people realize today that the samurai did not always draw a sword to quell a disturbance or to restore peace. It is quite true that the samurai regarded their two swords as symbols of their soul, an esteemed property. Also, they regarded the consciousness of shame as an essential of morality and their honor dearer than life itself. There were many times in the samurai's daily work that situations would develop, and his very presence would be considered so strong that his long sword would not need to be drawn to testify to his strength. Perhaps here can be observed the samurai's belief that "if your mind is clean and orderly, you will make your environment clean and orderly too."

The samurai would not blame an environment for failure or wrongdoing. These Japanese knights set the example for courageous enterprise and inspired self-confidence that continued for centuries. The samurai demonstrated that learning and spirituality are useless if they do not lead to practical attainments. With all of the pressures and frustrations bearing down upon modern man, these words of the samurai might be valuable: "Face nature and man, and learn."

The sternness of Bushido and its development of a direction for the feudal knights is still its outstanding characteristic. The sharpness of the contrast between Kamakura and Heian court life may serve as an illustrative point. At the Heian court the refinement of life was esteemed as much as it was in ancient Athens. The Kamakura court was similar to that of ancient Sparta, whose motto was "If not victorious, return on your shield."

Thus we can understand the people of Kamakura who exhorted their warriors going to battle to "receive arrows on your forehead, but never in your back." Frugality and chivalry were the precepts to inculcate the way of life among the youth who some day would be the defenders of the clan and later the country.

Notably, the samurai were men of action. They practiced plainness and economy. According to a Japanese proverb, when a hungry *bushi* was invited to eat, he would take out a toothpick and gratefully acknowledge that he was not hungry: *"Bushi wa kuwanedo, takayoji."* (Although the *bushi* has not eaten, he uses a toothpick.) Thus his remark would be of deep meaning. By his refusal he showed that he would not impose upon the kindness of friends who offered him scarce food.

As men of action the samurai were given to acting without any explanation, executing what they thought was justice. Their conduct is sometimes compared with that of men on the Western frontier of the United States during pioneer days. Among the favorite samurai maxims was "To know and to act are one and the same." Although they were men of attention to detail, they carried out their actions with dispatch. Yet there was a long course of training in preparedness for the moment of such action. Bushido held that the samurai was not to shed the blood of an opponent of unequal strength or of unequal rank. Yet the samurai felt at times called upon to sacrifice their most precious possession, whatever it might be, if it became necessary to do so for their lord or if it was within their duty.

Nevertheless, the samurai were not totally indifferent to life; indeed, they

35

had a great passion for life. They were extraordinarily inclined to see all that was good and honest, and they had a great eagerness to learn. Their personal honor of the spoken word was set above everything else. Poverty in the home was frequent, without being in any sense disgraceful, although they supported it with great difficulty.

The samurai asked questions and argued without knowing how to make an end of the matter. Eager to have an answer and to broaden their knowledge so that they could communicate to others what they had learned, they were constantly on the move throughout the land.

It should be no problem for the citizen or youth in modern society to see the virtue in such training. Of course, there is indeed much in the way of misunderstanding of a culture which demanded a strict adherence to a code like Bushido and carried this requirement into the 20th century.

It would indeed be regrettable to believe or to say that by adopting Bushido a person following such a strict code would find a better life. Nothing could be more far-fetched. To find a way of life means that one must be guided. The way of Bushido meant that through study and practice the road of life could be followed in a much clearer light. The person's knowledge of himself would become clearer and more meaningful.

Bushido as a code condemned action which was continued without correction, evaluation, or polish. There was always to be some improvement. The opportunities to make such corrections were noted, and action was taken. It was not to be put off. Reflecting on this ancient philosophy of life and its deep motivating force, which led men to train not only the body but the mind as well, one must be somewhat moved to study his own philosophy of life. The deep motivating force to train the mind becomes more meaningful to the person who wishes to avail himself of an opportunity to follow a more serene life in this world.

If nothing more, the Westerner can observe that the final stress in Bushido was laid on the basic substance of its inspiration: hard work, understanding, training, and—above all—patience. Much can be learned here if one will but adapt himself to the opportunity of learning how to have patience.

This severe training was carried out to the very letter of the unwritten code. Thus the time was exact for the rise of a new class in Japanese society, the samurai. These men did not hail, however, from an alien race or a newly risen class. The samurai were moulded out of a people who had served the aristocracy during the peaceful Nara and Heian periods.

Kamakura, during the former half of the feudal age, from the 12th century onward, was the center of a political organization of the samurai class and thus became the birthplace of the samurai movement in Japan.

The historical background of the samurai should be introduced here briefly to point out that they had their origin in the farming class and ascended the social ladder by serving either as subordinate bureaucrats of the aristocracy, police officers for the imperial court, or local administrative officials serving in the central government. The samurai were not from the merchant class, nor at any time did they come from the merchant class.

The age of the great swordsmen

During this early organization of the nation the art of *kenjutsu* became fully developed as a system of sword fighting. Nagahide Chujo (*fl.* 1380) founded the Chujo-ryu school of fencing. The Chujo family had served the Kamakura shogunate for generations, and Nagahide succeeded his father Yorihira and became a councilor of the shogunate.

Yoshimitsu Ashikaga (1358–1408) became the third shogun of the Ashikaga dynasty, and it was during this period that he became an admirer of Nagahide's skill as a swordsman. The special skill of Nagahide earned him the title of master swordsman of the clan under the shogun.

The best *kenjutsu* techniques were sought by each samurai who desired to perfect his fencing technique so that he might be invited to become a vassal of one of the most powerful lords. When a samurai reached near perfection and developed a special sword technique, he could open a fencing school and retire in his new-found life.

The imposing list of the great fencers of Japan reminds one of the lists of the famous European battles carried on by the crusaders in their long march to the Middle East. Feats of the Japanese knight or samurai equaled those of his counterpart in the West, thousands of miles away. The European knight drove across many nations, whereas in the case of the samurai it was a constant civil war.

37

6. Toshiro Mifune, Japan's leading actor of international fame, displays samurai virtuosity with his sword in a sequence from the film "Sanjuro" (Figs. 6–12, courtesy of Toho Company Ltd.). We see him here walking slowly into the face of death, fearless, with his hands inside his kimono to keep them warm. Such abandonment of caution throws his would-be attackers off guard.

The similarities between the feudal periods of Japan and Europe apply to armor, castles, weapons, and horsemanship, but the difference is in the style of fighting, the training of the warrior, and the philosophy or code of conduct in combat. The difference that is quite paramount and that sets the Japanese samurai apart from the European knight is the fact that the samurai gave little thought to defensive armor. Offensive armor was designed to protect the warrior and yet enable him to carry the attack to the opponent. Although there seems to have been no communication between the two feudal civilizations, both the European knight and the Japanese samurai had the same basic idea about armor. Armor was to cover the vital parts of the body and to afford the wearer protective cover in the course of battle. The armor worn by the kings and knights of Europe was made of plates covering the entire body of the wearer. The early knights of Japan made their armor out of bamboo and hide, woven together in the form of a mat that was quite flexible and light and yet afforded protection to the wearer. It is often said that European armor was realistic whereas Japanese armor was quite artistic.

There has been a common error held by many that the armor of the early European knights was discarded because of the development of firearms, which could reach the knight from beyond the range of his lance or

38

7. In a flash his left hand (not the customary right) draws the long sword from the scabbard, and a thrust to the rear stops the first assailant.

8. Drawing the sword out of the luckless assailant, he switches it to his right hand, and in one continuous sweep eliminates the two attackers who are charging in from the right.

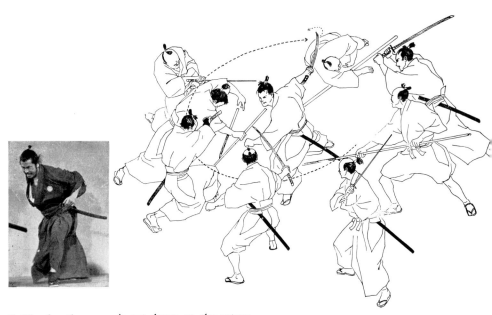

9. The fourth enemy is cut down on the return sweep of Mifune's sword before the opponent can even draw his.

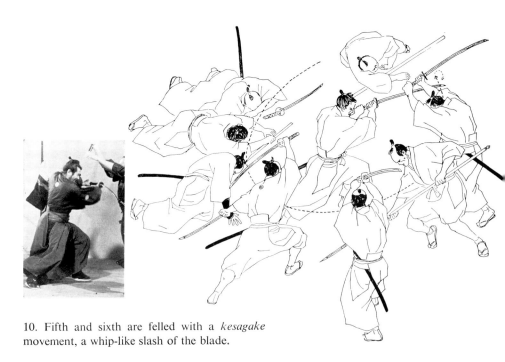

10. Fifth and sixth are felled with a *kesagake* movement, a whip-like slash of the blade.

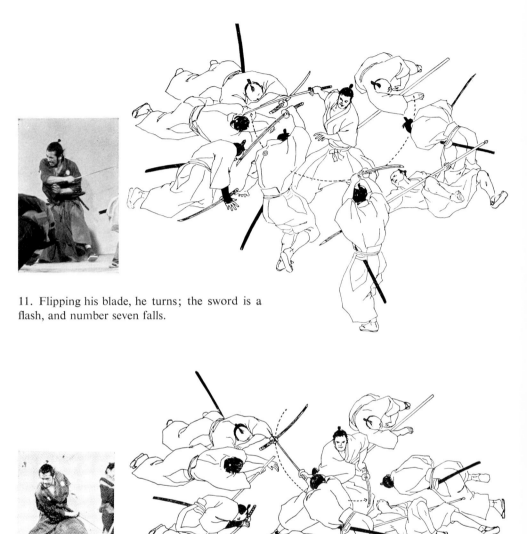

11. Flipping his blade, he turns; the sword is a flash, and number seven falls.

12. The remaining foe, the eighth, is quickly taken care of with a slashing *do-giri* stroke, the specialty of the swordsman. Standing, now, in the middle of the pile of his felled adversaries, he quietly returns his sword to the scabbard, the guard making a faint click as it strikes home. The whole action took no more than five seconds.

41

long sword. However, it was the introduction of the rifle in the hands of the foot soldier—who took careful aim and fired within range with improved powder and shot—which ended the role of the knight. Some armor could give the wearer protection against small arms and even against some ball and shot.

The paramount reason for the decline in armor was the development of new manuals on the martial arts calling for strategy in warfare. Wearing protective armor was excellent when riding out from the castle gate for a mile or so and then returning after a battle. The long marches and the maneuvering of armies on the field for a full day made the wearing of heavy armor much more difficult and tiring than the actual combat itself. Man and horse in heavy harness were easy prey to the fleet-footed infantryman who could outrun the overburdened beast.

An additional point for consideration is that in England there was no real armorer until the arrival of Henry II, who found that he had to order his suit of armor from the continent. Only the aristocratic class could afford the great suit of armor, and very few complete suits were made in comparison to the large numbers of knights who fought in Europe. The wearing of armor was continued until the middle of the 18th century and the wearing of the helmet by cavalry until modern times.

The rise of arms in Japan indicated a different philosophy of warfare. The sword was considered the principal weapon, and full attention was given to its use in all training. The various techniques on how to deliver a specific cut, blow, or thrust were mastered in a fencing school or *dojo*. Generally there was a *dojo* attached to a castle or one near at hand where a master swordsman would give such needed instruction.

The Japanese long sword or *katana* was the basic weapon and could be wielded by one or both hands at close quarters. The difference between the Japanese samurai and the European knight was the position of the body in combat. The European knight utilized his body and sword together. His long sword enabled him to keep himself a good distance away from his opponent. Sometimes the European long sword would be nine feet in length. Armed with such a weapon, the European knight could protect himself and yet make it possible to close with the enemy and not endanger his person too greatly.

42

In contrast to the European knight the Japanese samurai faced his enemy with the *katana* clutched in both hands—the right hand above the left—and opposed him with his body squarely to the front, with the right foot forward and the left foot drawn back. The point of the blade would generally be held directly in line with the opponent's throat.

This frontal position—facing the enemy with the sword—was a basic point of the Bushido training. It was the way-of-life spirit. The samurai trained his mind to hold this position with cool patience, maintaining it until the opponent could no longer stand the pressure and, under the strain of suspense, would make the first move in the attack.

The correct use of the sword was a major part of the training which a samurai received. However, it was the intense mental training that was highly regarded and was such a sought-after value in the *dojo*. This was the reason for searching out the strongest teacher who had acquired knowledge of this trait.

Inspecting Japanese swords of the past 1,500 years, from the time when the first sword was introduced into Japan from China, one notes that the shape of the sword underwent very slight modifications. One of the most authoritative texts on the subject is the handbook, *The Samurai Sword,* by John M. Yumoto, which states that in the Nara period swordmaking was still primitive but that swords were being furnished by the supporters of the Taika Reform. This marks the beginning of the Japanese sword.

The blade of the European sword constantly underwent changes in each historical period, as did the knight's armor. There was little change in the Japanese blade, however, and the sword would be handed down from one generation to the next with little sense of change in the shape of the blade. Even in the 20th century there are still families who have such a treasured heirloom: a sword used in the days of feudalism, a famous name of some six or eight centuries ago.

The Japanese *katchu* (armor) was designed for fighting on foot as well as on horseback. Such armor was not burdensome like the European plate harness, and although it was light and flexible, it proved to be just as protective in battle.

While the European headdress covered the entire head, the Japanese *kabuto* (helmet) covered only the crown and the nape of the neck. Partially

43

made of metal, it was given many coats of lacquer and was highly ornamented. To secure the helmet to the head, it was tied under the chin with two *himo* (cords). This method of securing the helmet led to the famous samurai motto enjoining constant alertness: "After victory, tighten your helmet cords!" *(Katte, kabuto no o o shime yo!)* The complete suit of armor, which was tied together with cords, was called *katchu* or full armor. When speaking of the helmet only, one identifies it as the *kabuto*.

Only the generals and warriors of high rank in the clans were allowed to wear the *yoroi* or great armor. Such armor can be obtained today in various parts of Japan, although there is some question as to its being the real armor or a copy.

The harness worn by the elite consisted of a helmet, large shoulder and arm protectors, hand covers, a chest protector, shin guards, and a hip protector. Shields were used not against enemy swords but against arrows in battle.

The period of the great armor began during the early 10th century and continued throughout the 12th century. These were the centuries that saw the rise of the large military clans in Japan and the spread of continual strife, leading to the long and bitter struggle between the Minamoto and the Taira.

For freedom of maneuver in battle the samurai's hands were always at liberty to use his *katana* or long sword, and if he was skillful, the long and the short sword were used at the same time. Hand-to-hand combat on the Japanese scale required the lightness of protective equipment because of the long marches over rugged terrain and the swift attack demanded of the warrior.

In the latter part of the 13th century Shigenobu Hayashizaki, second son of Yasutoki Hojo, founded a new kind of school of swordsmanship. His school introduced the new technique of rapidly drawing the long blade from the *saya* (scabbard), and Hayashizaki gave the new method the name of Shimmeimuso-ryu or Muso-ryu. This return of the art of drawing the sword blade as rapidly as possible was becoming popular for many reasons. The samurai now discovered that the change in wearing the long and the short sword tucked into the obi on the left side with the cutting

44

edge upward allowed the swordsman to draw his blade and to cut with a one-motion stroke.

The new technique soon became vital in swordsmanship, and its popularity was instrumental in bringing about a return to the form of *iai:* the sword exercise embodying a series of cutting and thrusting movements in drawing and returning the blade. One of Hayashizaki's outstanding students was Hisayasu Katayama, who later originated the Hoki school of swordsmanship, which continued to improve on the Muso-ryu technique.

In the Muromachi period (1336–1568) Kagehisa Ittosai Ito achieved a country-wide reputation as the strongest swordsman. Nobody could stand against him in combat with real swords, and he is honored as a unique swordsman in Japanese kendo history. Besides his superlative sword technique, his deep philosophical ideas and his experience of life are highly respected. He perceived the truth that all creatures are deductive from and inductive to one origin and that one sword technique multiplies into a million manipulations and all techniques ascribe to the original one technique of *kiriotoshi.* On the basis of this theory he named himself Ittosai (one-sword man) and formed the Itto-ryu (one-sword school) for his teaching lineage. The Itto-ryu flourished throughout the Tokugawa period and has survived up to the present time. Ittosai's excellent followers have included such important figures as Nobunaga Oda, Hidetada Tokugawa, Iemitsu Tokugawa, and many other feudal lords and shoguns—and even instructors of the present Tokyo Metropolitan Police Office. Modern kendo has been and still is strongly influenced by Itto-ryu.

During the 15th century some of the most skillful master swordsmen opened fencing schools to provide training for those who had joined the clans as vassals. Bungoro Hikida (1437–?), a famous swordsman and nephew of Kamiizumi Ise no Kami, in his later years served as a vassal to the Lord of Karatsu in Kyushu. Hikida went under various names such as Kagekane and Shohaku. His fencing technique was called the Hikida or Hikida-kage school. Two of his fencing pupils, Fugetsusai Yamada and Shimpachi Nakai, became famous swordsmen in later years.

A master teacher of a fencing school, when he reached a point in his life where he could no longer win matches or defeat his pupils, would retire to some secluded mountain area to spend the remaining days of his life in writing or reflective thinking. Some would utilize such a retreat to devise a new sword technique.

Iko Aisu (1452–1538) was an example of this problem of advancing age. However, during his secluded life in a cave in the Udo Shrine area of Miyazaki Prefecture, he was inspired to create a new school of swordsmanship. In 1488 he returned to open the Aisu-kage school and began to give instruction in a new fencing technique. His style of fencing was passed on to the father of Hidetsuna Kamiizumi and later greatly influenced the Yagyu, who were to be distinguished swordsmen in the building of Japan.

The founder of the Tenshin Seiden Shinto school of swordsmanship was Choisai Iizasa, who resided in Iizasa, Shimo-osa Province, which today is Chiba Prefecture. He gained great skill in all of the arts and was given the name of Yamashiro no Kami Ienao because of his excellent swordsmanship and the fact that he was considered a very capable and loyal samurai. Although he later became dissatisfied, took the vows of a Buddhist priest, and changed his name to Choisai, he continued to study *kenjutsu* at the Shinden school located at the Kashima and Katori shrines, both of which are dedicated to the martial deities. Later he developed his own school, training such swordsmen as Ichiu Moro-oka (originator of the Ichiu school), Tsukahara Tosa no Kami, and Masanobu Matsumoto.

Many stories have been written about Bokuden Tsukahara (1490–1572), who was raised in the village of Tsukahara, Ibaraki Prefecture. Bokuden learned *kenjutsu* from his father Kakuken Urabe, who was a Shinto priest at the Kashima Shrine. Another well-known swordsman who taught the young Bokuden was the above-mentioned Kamiizumi Ise no Kami, who developed a special technique for the use of the long blade. Young Bokuden learned his fencing lessons well and within a few years became one of the best swordsmen of his time. It is said that he undertook thirty-seven challenges without being defeated. His skill was due to the great stress he placed on mastering the various techniques and on concentration. These traits he displayed in his teaching of the fine points of swordsmanship in the fencing hall. He was a strong advocate of learning patience.

As Bokuden declined in years, he noticed that his technique was still sharp, although his former dexterity in the use of the blade was fading. This slowing down because of age, together with his great pride in his skill as a swordsman, led him to retire from his fencing school to a retreat in the mountains where he undertook a period of self-reflection and study.

Many young samurai sought him out in his mountain retreat for guidance and instruction in the art of swordsmanship. Such withdrawal from the pressures of daily living to think and to evaluate past actions and to reason the why of each past action is quite valuable for man to consider even today.

When such men lived by the skill of their fencing techniques, it is quite understandable why the philosophy of Zen would be followed by so many who searched for understanding. The beginner in kendo should realize that Zen is the silent contemplation of life and that kendo in feudal times was the movement of Zen or the action of life.

It should be noted that Bokuden Takamiki Tsukahara, who became a master of the blade and later a stoic, lived to be eighty-three years of age, dying a natural death in the third year of Genki (1572).

From the village of Yagyu in Yamato Province, which is today Nara Prefecture, came a young man by the name of Muneyoshi Yagyu (1527–1606). He began his fencing studies under the able guidance of Kamiizumi Ise no Kami, who founded the Shin-kage school. The young Muneyoshi soon became a capable swordsman, and through his service to two great feudal lords, Nobunaga Oda and Ieyasu Tokugawa, he was to become the shogun's fencing master. Because of his great character and his fencing skill he was given the title of Tajima no Kami, and he later established the Yagyu school of fencing, which soon became one of the most famous *dojo* in Japan.

His son, Munenori Yagyu (1571–1646) became an apt student under the able guidance of his father. A few years later Munenori became fencing instructor to Shogun Ieyasu Tokugawa, following in his father's footsteps. After the battle of Sekigahara (between Ieyasu Tokugawa and Hideyori Toyotomi) the young Munenori was granted a fief in Yamato Province with an annual yield of 2,000 *koku* (about 10,000 bushels) of rice and in addition was made governor of Tajima Province. Later, because of his

47

excellent record as an administrator, he was appointed *ometsuke* (chief of police) to the shogunate. Munenori Yagyu's life history has been made into many novels and motion-picture scripts.

Of the three master swordsmen during the latter part of the 16th century —Izu no Kami Jingo, Tsunenaga Hasekura, and Kazuyasu Ban—the most noted was Tsunenaga Hasekura (1571–1622). Hasekura was selected along with 68 followers to travel to Spain and Italy. He arrived in Spain in January 1615 and was given an audience with Philip III and later, in Italy, met Pope Paul V. The official party returned to Japan in 1620. During the entire trip Hasekura carried his two swords and also kept a notebook log of his various experiences.

One of the most popular swordsmen to come out of the pages of Japanese feudal history is Musashi Miyamoto (1584–1645). Miyamoto's recent popularity in the Western world results from the realistic film portrayal— based upon careful research—given of him by Toshiro Mifune, Japan's brilliant actor of samurai roles. Eiji Yoshikawa, one of Japan's most popular writers, gave the legend of Miyamoto renewed fame in his four-volume novel, *Miyamoto Musashi*. Some records state that Miyamoto was born in the town of Mimasaka in Okayama Prefecture, but contradictory records give his birthplace as Harima Province (now Hyogo Prefecture).

It is known that his father, Munisai Shimmen, was a noted fencing teacher who taught the art of *kenjutsu* to his son Masana, as Musashi was called before he left home and changed his name. Musashi was an apt student of his father's skill and soon became a strong fencer. Within a few years he became famous for his bold fencing technique. Records point out that during his life he engaged in sixty duels without losing a single one. Many of the most able fencers sought Musashi out to test their sword skill against his renowned technique. During his early life he met one of the most famous fencers, Kempo Yoshioka, and engaged in a duel with him in Kyoto. Over the years of early training Musashi developed a strong character and appeared to care little for his fame as a swordsman. He was quite intent on searching for perfection. Musashi appeared to hold his technique as imperfect and did not seem satisfied with his skill, for he continued his training throughout his life. He appeared to be very strong-willed. At the same time he achieved skill in various arts as well, especially in calligraphy and painting. His rare woodblock-printed book, *Gorin no Sho* (A Book of Five Rings), is a valuable discourse on mental discipline. The special technique that Musashi devised for the long and the short sword became the famous Niten-ichi-ryu of fencing.

In 1580 Musashi opened his Emmei school of two swords. He had become one of the most popular but feared fencers in the country. The Emmei technique that he fashioned for fighting required that the *daito* or long sword be held in the right hand and the short sword in the left. In the attack with the two swords the movement required that the long sword would cut first and the short sword would make a short slash or thrust. This style became a great challenge for the young fencers of the day. Lord Hosokawa noted the great skill of Musashi and soon requested his services as the master fencing teacher of the castle. Musashi died a natural death in 1645 at the age of sixty-one.

Another colorful fencer was Ganryu Sasaki, a retainer of the Mori clan in Aki Province, which today is Hiroshima. Sasaki evolved a fencing technique of his own which was suggested to him by the swift flight of swallows as they flitted about in the willow trees. Sasaki carried an unusually long sword which he referred to as his "clothes pole." In Harima Province Sasaki was defeated in a fencing match by Munisai Shimmen. Later Sasaki murdered Munisai out of chagrin for his fencing defeat at Munisai's hand.

Musashi Miyamoto soon learned of the murderous attack on his father and set out in search of Ganryu Sasaki to avenge his father's death. As it is recorded, Musashi finally caught up with his sworn enemy years later. Sasaki was killed by Musashi in the famous duel on the beach at Ganryu-jima in Kyushu. This noted vendetta is celebrated in *kodan* (feudal romances) and popular fiction, as well as in many versions that have appeared on the modern screen. Some sources indicate that the duel was only an ordinary fencing match in which Musashi defeated Ganryu.

Another revenge story that continues to be retold today in Kabuki drama, motion pictures, and popular paper-back editions comes from the life of Mataemon Araki (1594–1637). Mataemon was the founder of the Araki school of swordsmanship. He was born in Iga Province and in his early youth received training and instruction in the martial arts under the guidance of Mitsutoshi Yagyu. He soon became skilled in fencing and later was appointed fencing master to Honda Kai no Kami, daimyo of Koriyama in Yamato Province (now Nara Prefecture). He married the elder sister of Kazuma Watanabe, a retainer of Lord Ikeda of Bizen Province (Okayama Prefecture). Mataemon's involvement in a vendetta came about because Kazuma's younger brother, Gendayu, was killed in a duel by Matagoro Kawai. Kazuma and Mataemon avenged Gendayu by killing Matagoro. After the vendetta Mataemon and Kazuma served Lord Ikeda, who gave Mataemon a substantial award for his excellent swordsmanship.

The eldest son of Tajima no Kami Munenori was Mitsuyoshi Yagyu (1607–50). This famous member of the Yagyu family is known in literature, on the stage, and on the screen by his nickname of Jubei. Mitsuyoshi served the shogun Iemitsu Tokugawa as an agent on several missions to report on the activities of the daimyo in Kyushu. He founded a school of fencing at Masakizaki in Iga Province (Mie Prefecture). He is considered to be the real founder of the famous Yagyu school of kendo. Of the many forms of sword fighting devised in this period, the Yagyu form is considered to be one of the most formidable. The exploits of Mitsuyoshi have been dramatized in the feudal romance, *Yagyu Tabi Nikki* (A Travel Diary of Yagyu).

During this period of Japanese feudal history, Masayuki Hoshina (1611–72) should be given a place in any coverage of Bushido. The third son of the second Tokugawa shogun, he was adopted as heir by Sadamitsu Hoshina. Masayuki realized that the tenets of Bushido required loyal retainers to follow their masters in death. He decided to prohibit this practice. In his search for knowledge he invited the famous Confucian scholar Ansai Yamazaki to accept a post in his castle. Yamazaki arrived and was given the title of Confucian advisor. It is believed that Masayuki was greatly influenced by his advisor's wisdom in the matter of prohibiting retainers from sacrificing their lives upon their master's death.

Not all of the samurai followed the tide of battle or continued as followers of the martial arts. Hikozo Hirata (1626– ?), of Higo Province in Kyushu, turned from the rigorous life of a retainer to one of manufacturing the *tsuba* or guard for the sword. His designs were excellent, and he turned out *tsuba* of copper and brass with extraordinary skill. Much of his work is still to be admired in private and public collections.

In 1630 the name of Kurando Marume ranked among those of the four great swordsmen of the period. The other three were Izu no Kami Jingo, Bungoro Hikida, and Yagyu Tajima no Kami. It is written that Kurando served as a samurai from the province of Kozuke (Gumma Prefecture) at the Imperial Palace in Kyoto. Later he opened a fencing school at Asakusa in Edo. In a match held before Shogun Iemitsu Tokugawa in 1632 Kurando defeated many of the outstanding swordsmen of the day. At the end of the tournament, with the contestants using the *bokken,* Kurando tied Matabei Takada, the noted spearman, only to be defeated in turn by Bungoro Hikida. Having established himself as a master swordsman, however, Kurando opened a Shinkan-style swordsmanship school and gave instruction in the style that had won so many matches for him.

Two of the most famous *ryu* during the early Edo period were the Ono Itto-ryu (one-sword style) and the Arima Tessen. There were, of course, many others that were not as famous. The Ono Itto-ryu form of fencing is considered to have been developed during the latter part of the 17th century by Tadaaki, (Jirouemon) Ono disciple of Ittosai Ito. Earlier, Yagyu Tajima no Kami Muneyoshi (1527–1606) had reached a kind of culmination in the fencing style called the Yagyu Shin-kage. In general the style was a series of bold cuts and slashes with the blade held in a special ready position.

Zesuiken Iba (*fl.* 1690), Kanshin Teranishi (*fl.* 1700), and Tadaaki Ono (d. 1708) devised various techniques of fencing with the long sword, and it is notable that all three were interested in making changes in the method of fencing of the time. The reason for their concern in changing the style and affording protective armor for each fencer during the practice period was that many fencers were being killed or permanently disabled by serious injuries that occurred in the vigorous practice sessions.

The refinement of kendo

It remained for Chuta Nakanishi (*fl.* 1750), follower of Jirouemon Ono and founder of the Nakanishi Itto-ryu, to make the most significant contributions toward kendo weapons and armor (Fig. 13). At his school the one-sword technique was taught, and at the same time a change was made in the method of instruction. During Chuta's student days at the *dojo* of Chuichi Ono IV he was considered a much better fencer than his teacher. His respect for his teacher caused him to leave the school to establish one of his own. He carried away with him a dissatisfaction over the use of the dummy sword that Ono had invented to take the place of the dangerous live blade used in battle as well as in practice. Although Chuta realized the many advantages of the dummy sword and wished to improve on Ono's design and theory, it took years of experimentation.

One of the greatest strides in developing protective armor for the practice session was Chuta's invention of the *kote* or fencing glove. His second improvement was the redesign of the dummy sword invented by his teacher. The new-style *shinai* or fencing foil (see Fig. 18) was made out of bamboo reeds. A strict disciplinarian in his *dojo,* he demanded that all of his students use both the *kote* and the *shinai* during their informal practice sessions. Many students did not approve of the new armor and left. However, there were many who saw the advantage in the fact that if a fencer could concentrate on his technique entirely without the slightest thought of injury to his opponent when he struck him with all his power, a large degree of realism would be achieved by such action. By the time Chuta III was teaching at the same *dojo* the *shinai* was generally accepted by most fencing teachers throughout Japan.

In 1760 there were three types of sword training available to an aspiring young samurai who desired to perfect his skill or keep his proficiency at a high level. He could use the live blade *(katana)* in kendo *kata* (exercises), the *bokken* (solid wooden sword), or the new invention, the dummy sword called a *shinai.*

It was soon apparent that the ideal weapon had been invented, since each swordsman could now deliver a full blow without any concern of causing an injury. The samurai had freedom to deliver a blow and a slash utilizing the full technique of his special skill developed through long hours of training.

The first *shinai* was made by selecting soft reeds which were split into sixteen to thirty-two strips and covered with a heavy cloth. There was a need to make the *shinai* have approximately the same weight as a real sword or a *bokken.* The sense of realism was apparent, for the fencer could deliver a blow, and the opponent could block the blow or attack.

52

13. The kendo armor. Top to bottom: the *men;* the *do,* with the right and left *kote* on either side; the *tare;* and the *shinai* to the right (the left of the person wearing the armor).

Between 1765 and 1770 the development of additional protective equipment for the fencer in the *dojo* was undertaken. Chuzo Nakanishi of Edo continued with his search for a complete fencing armor. His next design was the chest protector, called a *do,* to be used with the *kote* and the *shinai.* This piece of equipment further improved the practice period for a fencer, removing any inhibition of holding back from fear of injury to his opponent.

Soon Nakanishi had designed an improvement over the first reedlike *shinai.* The new dummy sword was made out of four selected and well-balanced sections of highly polished bamboo. The sections were fitted together to form a cylindrical weapon and tied in place with leather strips. A *tsuba* or guard made of thick hide was fitted on the handle of the *shinai.*

Originally there were no rules or regulations established beyond those in use for the *katana* or the *bokken.* There had been no limitation on the length or the weight of the *shinai.* Some were over six feet in length, and Susumu Oishi, a famous fencer, is recorded as having used a six-and-a-half-foot *shinai* with great skill in a match.

Now Nakanishi's *fukuro shinai,* as it was called, was adopted, and its regulation length was established as not more than 38 or 39 inches and its weight as less than three pounds. This special weapon afforded free action to the arms and allowed the fencer unlimited opportunity to move in a coordinated fighting action without any simulated action.

The *hakama* (divided skirt) and the *keikogi* (jacket) were standard wearing apparel in and out of the fencing hall. The next piece of protective equipment was the *tare,* made of heavy quilted cotton and designed for hip and groin protection. The *tare* was the first piece of fencing equipment to be placed outside the *hakama,* followed by the *do* or chest protector. This *tare* or waistband fitted snugly around the body and was held in place by two bands that tied in front under its center flap. The *tare* was designed with five flaps or pendants—three large and two small—about 12 inches in length.

In fitting the *do* or chest protector above the *tare,* the kendoist crossed the *himo* or cords in back and brought them down to the loops on the two crests of the *do* in front. The bottom cords of the *do* were always tied loosely in order to allow the *do* some freedom of movement.

54

The most advanced piece of equipment for the fencer was the *men* or head-and-face mask. With this piece of equipment, he was protected from the full force of a blow on the top or the side of the head. The *men* was constructed with a steel face guard set in protective cotton lining. Forehead and chin guards of softer material were included in the padding. The *men*, like all kendo equipment except the *kote* or protective mitts, was tied on with two cords secured to the steel ribs of the face guard. These cords were wrapped around the head and tied in the back and to the side of the neck. Generally under the *men* the kendoist wore a cotton towel, called a *tenugui* or *hachimaki*, to keep the perspiration from running down into his eyes and to protect the back of his neck from chafing by the cords of the *men*.

This protective armor required a new set of rules for the *dojo*, and the new style of fencing came to be called kendo. The word *ken* 剣 means sword, and the word *do* 道 means the way. When the two characters are placed together they form kendo, the way of fencing or the way of the sword. Kendo regulations will be discussed in detail in the second part of the book.

With the improvement of equipment and the organization of specific rules of conduct in the *dojo*, the fencing schools began to flourish, and eventually there were some 300 positions developed for the swordsman with protective equipment. By 1780 there appeared to be some discussion about narrowing down the various forms to a much smaller number. Soon after this period the positions were refined and revised so that the fencing masters could select 100 positions to be considered throughout the fencing schools of Japan.

Thus freed by the use of the *fukuro shinai* and the new armor from the danger of permanent injury, the samurai were able to carry on the practice of striking and thrusting in a realistic manner. In 1871 the Japanese Ministry of Education passed a regulation that made kendo compulsory in all public and private schools in Japan. Emphasis was placed on the mental, moral, and physical value of training in an ancient martial art. Character building was the purpose of introducing kendo into the classroom. Kendo was slowly becoming a sport, and many schools organized kendo clubs outside of school. The techniques of kendo were taught by famous kendo masters who extended the activity beyond the academic field into various business and industrial companies, and both private- and government-operated *dojo* were established wherever space could be found. The Japanese police used both kendo and judo as a means of keeping in excellent physical and mental condition as well as a means of developing a strong spirit of comradeship.

Modern kendo

The Meiji (1868–1912) government suffered several setbacks in its modernization plans through the Saga rebellion in 1876 and the Kumamoto rebellion in 1878, and again in the struggles of the Shugetsu and the Hagi rebellions. Because of these samurai uprisings it appeared that a ban on the use of the sword would be issued by the central government. As anticipated, the ban was soon passed, and it strictly forbade the wearing or the use of any sword in public by anyone in the old capital of Kyoto.

At the same time, Koseki, an ardent teacher of kendo who lived at Kameoka-machi in Kyoto (later to become the headquarters of kendo in Japan), gathered relatives and students for kendo practice. Through his teaching, the various styles and techniques were passed on for future generations to follow. Once Koseki was arrested for giving instruction in the sword and was imprisoned in the Nijo Castle for six months as punishment.

Although *kenjutsu* was barely able to exist in the new society, the public had not completely abandoned the ancient art. There were many people scattered throughout Japan who continued to have a deep interest in the preservation of the various *ryu* or styles. At Kameyama in Ise, for example, the Riemon Yamazaki *dojo* taught the Shinryoto form, and at the famous Tobukan in Mito (Ibaraki Prefecture) Torakichi Ozawa gathered the local students together and taught them the Hokushin Itto-ryu kendo. Here Takahara Naito, Shigeyoshi Takano, Toshitada Hiyama, and other famous kendoists gathered to instruct in the art of fencing. The Tobukan *dojo* has continued to this day, and it is now under the direction of Takeshi Ozawa, who holds fencing classes daily. Over 200 juvenile kendoists *(shonenkenshi)* practice every day at the Tobukan *dojo* and later continue their training at junior high school, high school, and college.

There were other fencing halls that existed with difficulty because of the lack of support, but the authorities did not interfere with their activities, since they were endeavoring to teach kendo as a sport. The civilian fencing halls gradually became extinct, and Japanese Bushido, with a heritage of a thousand or more years, was slowly fading away. Yet *kenjutsu,* now becoming the sport of kendo, was kept alive by the encouragement given the new art by the Japanese police force and by Kenkichi Sakakibara (1830–94), who aroused and fostered interest among the people by sponsoring fencing exhibitions for a small admission fee. Such efforts were the starting point for the revival of kendo schools in the latter part of the Meiji period.

Others, like Tesshu Yamaoka and his Muto-ryu (swordless school), continued to offer training in fencing. Tesshu Yamaoka was considered to be the foremost swordsman during the early Meiji period, when kendo and other military arts were on the wane. At the time when civilian practice halls were declining in popularity, Yamaoka maintained a practice hall and trained many young men in fencing. During his lifetime kendo slowly started to flourish as a sport. When Yamaoka died in 1888, his followers, Yasusada Koteda, Dotaro Takahashi, Seijitsu Nakata, Yasutomo Konami, and Zenjiro Kagawa, were well-known kendo teachers and exerted full efforts to make kendo flourish. Hiroichi Nishikubo, a student of Zenjiro Kagawa, after retiring from public life, opened his own fencing hall and trained many young swordsmen in his special techniques.

Supporting the kendo teachers in their desire to keep kendo alive was the organization of the Sword Unit of the Tokyo police force. The Metropolitan Police Bureau at one time had 6,000 members in this special force. The bureau strongly encouraged the continued practice of kendo and judo among the members of its organization.

As a result of the Meiji Restoration and the ban on wearing swords, the samurai were left without any source of income. The teachers of the various fencing schools throughout the country also had their revenue cut off by the same governmental order. In an effort to deal with their mutual problems and to aid these unemployed swordsmen, as well as to promote an interest in fencing with the hope of making it continue, Kenkichi Sakakibara once again gathered former samurai around him on the basis of their skill in the use of the sword. He presented a petition for the support

57

of his fencing exhibitions on the grounds that, because of hardships and difficulty in making a living, he would like to form a fencing company and conduct exhibitions throughout the country. He respectfully requested the Meiji government to grant him permission to carry out his program promptly. The government undertook to study his request, and on April 11, 1873, with its permission, the first fencing exhibition was opened in Asakusa, Tokyo. The most noted fencers, including Kiyotake Ogawa, Makoto Ozawa, and Shinkichi Nosé, appeared in this exhibition. All of the masters had been teachers of fencing under the *bakufu* (shogunate).

Noritoshi Matsudaira, Masateru Oda, and Shige Suzuki had the difficult task of handling exhibition arrangements, choosing future sites for matches, and creating publicity. The fencing exhibitions proved very popular with the public and were well received wherever the masters appeared. One of the reasons for such popularity was that the public, as commoners under the shoguns, had not been allowed to learn fencing—not to mention the fact that even to watch it had been forbidden. Therefore, by just paying a small admission price, everyone was welcome to watch only experts perform. Yet, in spite of this initial popularity, few became truly enthusiastic, and in time the interest in such fencing exhibitions waned.

Some were of the opinion that the exhibitions destroyed the spirit of fencing, while others said that they brought good results. The exhibition tours throughout the country did, however, foster an interest in kendo, and an increasing number of people began to enroll their children in kendo schools.

The first reference to the study of kendo by foreigners is found in the records of Sakakibara's fencing school at Kurumazaka in Tokyo. Sakakibara's demonstration of splitting a helmet with a sword, given in the presence of Emperor Meiji at the residence of Prince Fushimi in 1887, indicates the position that such fencers held with the government.

It is not difficult to realize the deep feelings that many people had upon entering the 20th century and reflecting back on the past thirty years, during which the Meiji Restoration had completely changed Japan. After the downfall of the Tokugawa shogunate the new Meiji government abolished the old system, and the entire country concentrated on absorbing the new culture of the advanced Western nations. Social customs, manners, education, and the caste system underwent a complete transformation. The samurai class, which had constituted the middle and guiding class of the masses, was abolished. In theory, at least, the Meiji constitution brought almost overnight an equality that had never existed before.

The samurai were forced to look elsewhere for their means of livelihood. Some turned to business; others continued their education, concentrating on the study of Western knowledge. Still others entered the military forces of the new government or turned to the police force for employment. Only a very small handful continued to pursue or maintain the martial arts of feudal Japan. With the restoration, everyone became so interested in Western culture that no one, except a few kendo teachers and some traditionalists, retained an interest in the former established customs, which now were suddenly considered old-fashioned and out of place. There were a few, as mentioned, who did believe that the art of kendo was an excellent physical and mental exercise and who approved of kendo as a sport in the new system of education.

On November 1, 1909, at Tokyo University, the first college kendo federation was formed. The promoter of this student federation was Noboru Watanabe, who was later elected first president of the All-Japan College Kendo Federation. In 1928 another kendo group was formed and organized into a federation. Later in the same year the All-Japan Kendo Federation was officially organized. This national federation gave membership to all professional and amateur kendo *dojo* and to any individual kendoist who passed a set of examinations at a *dojo*. Upon recommendation of his teachers, the federation would grant the individual kendoist a *dan* (grade or rank). The main purpose of the organization was to hold annual examinations and to grant kendo grades or *dan,* as well as to inspect the quality of teaching in the various fencing halls. Its guiding principle was the fostering of the ideals of kendo on a national and an international level.

The first president of the All-Japan Kendo Federation was Masataro Fukuda, who held this office for nearly twenty years. Under the leadership of President Fukuda the federation granted specific kendo degrees based upon specific recommendations.

At this point it is pertinent to say a word about the *dan* granted in kendo. The following list shows the *dan* in the ascending order of achievement, the *judan* or tenth grade being the highest.

This Is Kendo

Dan Granted in Kendo

judan	tenth grade
kudan	ninth grade
hachidan	eighth grade
shichidan	seventh grade
rokudan	sixth grade
godan	fifth grade
yodan	fourth grade
sandan	third grade
nidan	second grade
shodan	first grade

The beginner in kendo must advance through a series of six *kyu* or classes before he is eligible for the first dan. He is placed in the sixth *kyu* and progresses upward through the first, his progress depending upon many factors and the requirements of the particular *dojo*.

In modern kendo the advance through the six *kyu* will take anywhere from two to five years before the student can receive consideration for an examination by the board of teachers for the first-grade *(shodan)* examinations. It must be mentioned that each kendoist is ranked by *kyu* or *dan* and that age, height, weight, or position in life has little bearing on the presentation of a kendo grade. There are no honorary kendo grades or ranks, and the specific grades in which the kendoist is given special titles are those from four to six, in which he becomes a *renshi,* and those from eight to ten, in which he becomes a *hanshi.* To achieve such merit, the kendoist must produce some research and take an examination.

There are still outstanding exponents of the art of kendo in Japan who have viewed its transformation from an art of the sword to an art of the bamboo *shinai* (Fig. 14). Five of these men, all of whom have been met in matches by one or both of the authors, are introduced in the following paragraphs.

The first modern kendoist of the five was Kyutaro Takahashi, who was born in Himeji, Hyogo Prefecture, in 1858 and whose family for generations served as kendo instructors of the Sakai family of the Himeji clan. Even in his late nineties Takahashi continued to teach his Mugai-ryu kendo at his school in Hyogo Prefecture.

14. Some kendo notables. Dr. Junzo Sasamori (facing camera) engages J. Ono. Seated among the spectators in the front row are M. Mochida (first from left), G. Saimura (next to Mochida) and H. Nakayama (behind Sasamori holding a *shinai* in cloth wrapping).

Shigeyoshi Takano (1877–1957) was a student at the Mito Tobukan school of fencing and later became an exponent of the Itto-ryu. In a command duel before the present Emperor Hirohito, Takano was defeated by Moriji Mochida in the final match of the day.

Kinnosuke Ogawa (1884–) began his study of fencing in Aichi Prefecture, practicing the style known as Hokushin Itto-ryu and later joining the Butokukai in Kyoto. He was appointed instructor at the Military Arts School and by 1908 had established himself as an expert fencer. He is one of the most active sponsors of kendo as a sport.

In Gumma Prefecture, Zensaku Mochida began teaching his young son Moriji the fine points of kendo at an early age. Moriji Mochida (1885–) began his kendo schooling by entering the Bujutsu Kyoin Yoseijo (Fencing Instructor School) of the Kyoto Butokukai in 1907. He was employed by the Chiba Prefectural Department of Police in 1919 and later by the fencing section of the Tokyo Higher Normal School. In 1929, in the presence of Emperor Hirohito, he won the national kendo championship.

At present he is head of the Myogi Dojo in Tokyo and also serves with the Metropolitan Police Bureau. He has long been an advocate of kendo as a sport and has strongly supported Goro Saimura and Kinnosuke Ogawa in their efforts to make kendo a national sport. On November 9, 1961, Prime Minister Hayato Ikeda presented Mochida with the Cultural Medal.

Goro Saimura (1887–), of Fukuoka Prefecture, served as an instructor in kendo at the Miyazaki Middle School in Kyushu. In 1916 he became kendo instructor for the Tokyo Metropolitan Police Bureau, as well as kendo instructor at Waseda University.

Under the leadership of these men kendo has flourished not only in Japan but in other countries as well. There have been international team matches between the United States and Japan. Waseda University students, for example, have visited the United States for a series of kendo matches, and one of the most extensive kendo-team programs was that of the American team that traveled throughout Japan in 1940. In 1955 a group of Meiji University students met with teams on the west coast of the United States. In November 1956 an American kendo team under the leadership of Torao Mori *(hachidan)* and Yutaka Kubota *(godan)* left the United States for a four-week good-will tour of Japan (Fig. 5). The team met Japanese teams in Tokyo, Yokohama, Kyoto, and Osaka during its visit.

In the summer of 1957 a thirteen-man all-Japan university student kendo team was selected from universities throughout Japan to tour the United States in a series of kendo matches and to participate in a United States-Japan match at Long Beach State College on August 24. The team was led by Giichi Maruyama, of the personnel division of Hosei University; Eiichi Kijima, of Keio University; Masataka Inoue, of the Osaka municipal government; and Junzo Sasamori, one of the co-authors of this book. In 1960 four seventh-rank *(shichidan)* kendoists from the All-Japan Kendo Federation—Ichibara, Ogata, Oura, and Matsubara—visited various American fencing halls and, at Long Beach State College, thrilled capacity audiences with their skill.

Today kendo is a modern sport in Japan with such leaders as Diet members Tokutaro Kimura and Toshio Watanabe, and in the United States with such outstanding kendoists as Torao Mori and Yutaka Kubota, as well as others who have found in the sport of kendo a new way of life.

62

At the present time in Japan junior high school and high school students have kendo as an elective (Fig. 3). University kendo teams meet in annual championship matches for individual and team titles. No fewer than twelve annual kendo championship matches are held, as the list below shows. (Each group is listed in its rank position.)

1. All-Japan Championships
2. All-Japan University Student Championships
3. All-Japan Police Championships
4. All-Japan Industrial and Commercial Firms Championships
5. All-Japan Physical Education Championships
6. All-Japan Prefectural Championships
7. All-Japan Schoolteachers' Championships
8. Kyoto Championships (*godan* to *judan* grade)
9. All-Prefectural Junior High School Championships
10. All-Japan High School Championships
11. All-Japan Land Defense Force Championships
12. East and West Championships

With Brazil and other countries, like the United States, taking a greater interest in kendo as a sport, perhaps some day in the future annual international kendo championship matches will be held.

2

Kendo Equipment and Basic Rules

The dojo or fencing hall

There are general basic regulations for the construction of a *dojo,* and these are followed closely. The floor must be constructed of highly polished hardwood, carefully joined so as not to allow the possibility of exposed rough edges that might be hazardous to the barefooted kendoist. It must also be a flexible or floating floor in order to protect the kendoist from painful leg injuries—for example, in the rapid movements in which he often drives his right foot forward and smartly down in a series of drives to secure a point.

The *tatami* mats set into the floor along the sides of the *dojo* are used by the kendoists for a dressing area or a rest area during practice. They are also used by visitors who often drop in at the *dojo* to observe and enjoy the practice sessions.

The morning practice period held during the summer months is called the *asageiko,* while that of the winter months is known as *kangeiko.* A kendo practice session usually begins around 6 a.m. with the huge *taiko* (drum) calling the kendoists to the floor of the *dojo.* The session lasts from an hour and a half to two hours or more. The afternoon or evening practice is scheduled for the convenience of the students and is generally held between five and seven or between seven and nine in the evening.

There is much activity in the *dojo* prior to a practice period (Fig. 15). Equipment must be checked, and the *shinai* must be inspected to make sure that there is no protruding splinter or sharp edge that might harm the kendoists.

65

15. The *dojo* is a busy place before the practice starts. Members of the Hosei University kendo team preparing for a practice period. The characters on the *hachimaki* (towel wrapped on head to cushion the *men*) state that it is a memento from the national intercollegiate championships.

16. In a kendo *shiai* (match) there are three referees or judges—two forward and one rear. Two of the referees can be seen with their red and white flags.

17. The kendo hall must have a smooth wooden floor, and matches are held within an area of 27 to 33 feet square, delineated by a white line. This is the famed Mitsubishi Company's *dojo* during an early-morning practice session.

After the exercise period, tea and a hot bath are usually ready, and in some of the large company *dojo* breakfast is served as soon as the kendoist has taken a bath and changed his clothing. At such time one always hears the kendoists enthusiastically commenting on how refreshed they feel after practice.

There are many famous old fencing halls in Japan that have continued since feudal times. Many kendoists travel throughout the country, practicing at each fencing hall to improve their techniques and enjoying bouts with famous kendoists. The samurai word for this custom of visiting various dojo was *mushashugyo*, a term which might well be translated as knight-errantry.

Fencing area regulations

The regulations for a kendo practice or tournament area (Fig. 4) are very specific. They call for a smooth wooden-floored area 9 to 11 meters (27 to 33 feet) square. The boundaries must be marked with a white line 5 to 10 centimeters (2 to 4 inches) wide. An area of at least 3 meters beyond the line should be kept clear so that the line judges will have an unobstructed view of the foul lines.

The center of the fencing field must be marked with a circle or an X, and from this center point a starting line of 1.5 meters (4 feet, 6 inches) is drawn each way in the direction of the boundary line. The starting mark is a white line 1 meter (3 feet) long.

The contest field must be carefully inspected by one of the judges to insure that there are no splinters in the floor and that it is free from dirt and gravel.

Two foul-line flagmen will be located at opposite corners to notify the *shimpan* (referees) when the kendoist has stepped over the foul line. The foul-line flagmen will remove their chairs whenever they leave the fencing area after a match.

In a kendo *shiai* (match) there are three referees or judges—two forward and one rear (Fig. 16). When a point is scored, the forward judges raise their flags—either red or white, depending upon which kendoist has scored —to indicate the victory.

The etiquette of kendo

The regulations prescribed by kendo authorities are carefully followed in the social and official life of the kendoist. As a rule, each of these customs has been handed down from ancient times and is continued as a part of kendo. The following rules of etiquette are observed wherever kendo is taught.

1. Whenever a kendoist enters or leaves a *dojo,* he bows in greeting or farewell to those present.

2. A kendoist bows to his opponent at the start and finish of each practice.

3. A kendoist does not smoke in a *dojo* unless invited to do so.

4. A kendoist does not wear a hat in the *dojo.*

5. When kendoists are wearing *dogu* (fencing equipment) and are in a sitting position on the *dojo* floor, it is customary to walk in back of them. If for any reason one must walk in front of seated kendoists, he should extend his right hand and bow slightly as he passes.

6. A kendoist never steps over or hits a *shinai* with his feet when it is placed to the left of a seated kendoist or when the *kote* and *men* are placed in position on the floor.

7. A kendoist never touches the *dogu* of another kendoist.

8. Always upon entering or leaving the *dojo,* a kendoist greets or takes leave of the head teacher first.

9. Generally the beginners or kendoists of lowest rank will sit opposite the *yudansha* (higher grade holders) or to their right.

10. In a practice, the beginning kendoist takes his position facing the *yudansha.*

11. It is important to remember that the student always stands at the practice area and awaits the teacher's instruction.

12. If a piece of armor comes untied, practice must be stopped, and the opponent kendoist will remain in position while the repair is made and the equipment is finally inspected. In a match, time is called so that such repair can be made. When the opponents are ready to resume practice (or the match), each will stand and bow before continuing.

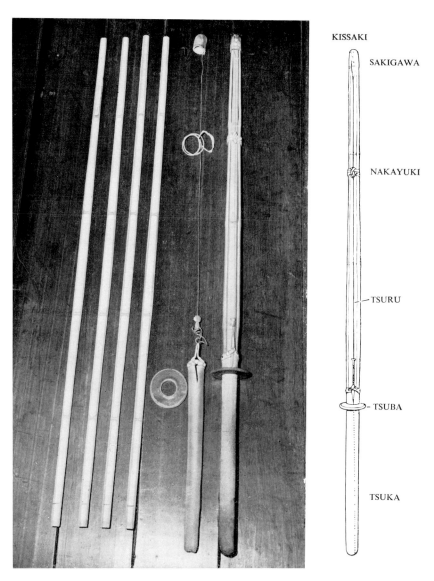

KISSAKI

SAKIGAWA

NAKAYUKI

TSURU

TSUBA

TSUKA

18. The *shinai* and its parts.

The shinai or fencing foil

The fencing foil or stave (Fig. 18) used in kendo is made of four well-seasoned, highly polished, and equally weighted sections of choice bamboo. The sections are matched so that there will be no dangerous edges to break or splinter. They are fitted together and held in place by the *sakigawa,* the *nakayui,* and the *tsuka,* at which points they are tied tightly and held together by the *himo* or string.

70

19. The kendo apparel and equipment.

The apparel and how it is worn

The first articles of apparel (Fig. 19) that the kendoist puts on are the *keikogi* (jacket) and the *hakama* (skirtlike trousers). The *keikogi* is either a light or a heavy hand-made quilted cotton jacket that can be blue, black, or white in color. This garment acts as a protection against bruising blows and at the same time absorbs perspiration. The *keikogi* should be loose-fitting and have freedom at the shoulders. The *hakama* is a divided skirt made of cotton material, the two sections serving as pants legs.

The *keikogi* is put on first and tied in place with a string on the right side. Next the kendoist steps into the *hakama*, draws it up around his waist, and ties it snugly in back. Then the strings attached to the *koshiate*, the stiff back section of the *hakama*, are brought around the waist and tied securely in front. The *keikogi* should then be straightened out and drawn into place, making sure that there are no wrinkles in the garment. The pleats of the

20. First, the kendoist puts on the *tare* or waist protector.

21. Then, the *do* or chest protector.

hakama should fall downward in a straight line. When the kendoist assumes the sitting position, the folds of the *hakama* legs should be spread out to each side.

The first piece of armor that the kendoist ties on is the *tare* or waist and hip protector, the name of which means hanging waist armor (Fig 20). The *tare* has two wide band-strings *(himo)* that hold the band onto the waist. The *tare* is hand-made of heavy cotton material, several layers of which are used in order to give it stiffness and enable it to serve as a protector. The *himo* are wrapped around the waist and tied securely in front under the large center flap, which serves not only to give protection but also to hide the *himo* knot. When the *tare* has been tied securely into place, the kendoist should stand up and, with his hands, curl first the left and then the right flap toward the front. This gives additional protection as well as a neat appearance to the *tare*.

The next piece of kendo armor is the *do* or chest protector (Fig 21). The *do* is made of strips of heavy bamboo lashed together in place vertically and then covered with a heavy hide to make it firm and hold the bamboo in place. Above this goes a leather cover to give additional support to the bamboo and extra protection to the area above the chest. The front cover of hide is given many coats of lacquer to afford a base for the high degree

22–23. The *hachimaki* is wrapped around the head.

of polish given to the *do*. As a rule, a kendoist will have a black *do* with a design on the upper part in color. Sometimes, however, the *do* will be red or will have a special design indicating that it was presented as an award or perhaps just reflecting the taste of the kendoist.

The *do* is tied on with two upper *himo* (strings) that are crossed left to right and right to left over the kendoist's shoulders. Each *himo* is then fastened to a leather loop at the right or the left peak of the *do* in front. The weight of the *do* should hang equally on each *himo*. The two short *himo* at the bottom of the *do* should be tied snugly in back to prevent the *do* from slipping forward.

Donning the *hachimaki* or *tenugui* is a prologue to putting on the *men*. The word *hachimaki* cannot be translated literally into English; the nearest translation means a towel-like cloth (Fig. 22). The *hachimaki* is generally made of cotton and is used to keep the perspiration off the brow and out of the eyes while the kendoist is wearing the *men*. It also serves as a minimum cushioning for the *men* in the case of blows on the head or the face guard, as well as a cushion for the *men himo* at the nape of the neck to keep the knot from cutting into the skin. The *hachimaki* is wrapped around the head in the manner shown in Fig. 23. The edges are tucked under, and the back is set at the nape of the neck.

24. And the *men,* the head guard, goes on.

25. And is firmly tied in the back, the wings of the *men* pulled out to make sure they are free from the *himo,* the binding cords.

Hachimaki are valued by all kendoists as mementos of the matches or contests in which they have participated. The *hachimaki* is usually given as a gift from a *dojo* to a visiting kendoist who uses its facilities for a practice session.

The next piece of kendo armor that the kendoist becomes familiar with is the *men* or face mask. Made of heavy cotton material with a heavy steel face protector, the *men* gives the head and face ample protection against any blow or thrust. The proper way to place the *men* on the head is first to open the wings back wide, spreading them apart so they will not push the *hachimaki* off the head. The lower front inside of the mask has a chin-rest piece that should be in line with the bottom of the chin. The *men* is then pushed on and back so that the top forehead and the chin fit securely on the forehead piece and the chin rest, the *hachimaki* acting as a buffer between the surface of the forehead and the protective pad in the *men* (Figs. 24–25).

Once the *men* is firmly secured on the head, the *himo* are drawn tightly from the top around the head and back through the mask. Generally the *himo* are wrapped around the *men* twice and drawn tight to make sure that each cord is above the ears. The knot is tied securely, and the cords are drawn out to equal length. The kendoist should make sure that the *himo*

74

26. The last items to be worn are the *kote*, the arm guards.
27. And the kendoist is ready for a bout.

and the knot are resting on the *hachimaki* so as to prevent irritating the skin. As a rule, the base attachment of the *himo* to the *men* should be in line with the mouth or about four bars upward on the *men* (Fig. 24).

The last item that the kendoist puts on is the *kote* (Fig. 26). It is important to remember that the *kote* should always be grasped by the sleeve area whenever it is being pulled on or pushed off. A kendoist never grasps the hand area of the *kote* to remove it. The pulling-on or pushing-off motion is made by firmly placing one hand on the forearm area of the *kote* and then withdrawing the other hand. If the hand area of the *kote* is used in withdrawing the hand, the forearm part will be stretched out of shape, and the seams around the hand area will be weakened. Both the right and the left *kote* are put on and removed in the same way.

The proper fit of the *kote* is very important, and the kendoist should always feel comfortable when he places the *shinai* in the palm area of the *kote*. The fingers should never feel cramped inside the hand area. After each practice the *kote* should be dried out with the leather palm turned downward. The *kote* should never be placed directly in the sun with the palm upward, since this will burn the leather and make it very hard.

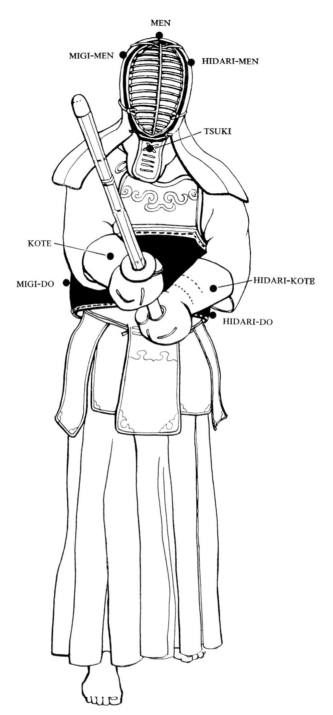

28. The point areas used in kendo.

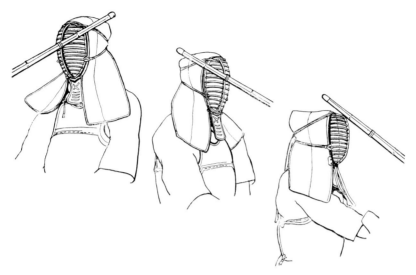

29. *Hidari-men:* a clean blow on the left side of the *men.*
30. *Migi-men:* a similar blow on the right of the *men.*
31. *Men:* a blow directly in the center of the head.

The point areas used in kendo

There are eight point areas which can be scored in kendo (Figs. 28–34): seven blows and only one thrust. The seven blows are considered to be cutting motions and are directed to the following points: (1) *hidari-men,* a point on the left side of the *men* just above the left ear; (2) *men,* a point directly at the peak of the face mask; (3) *migi-men,* a point on the right side of the *men* just above the right ear; (4) *kote,* a point just above the wrist joint on the right arm; (5) *hidari-kote,* a point on the left wrist, allowable only when the left hand is at shoulder height or higher; (6) *migi-do,* a point on the right side of the chest protector; (7) *hidari-do,* a point on the left side of the chest protector. The only thrust used in kendo is a lunge directed to the throat protector on the bottom of the *men* and called *tsuki.* The thrust may be carried out with both hands or with either the right or the left hand.

It is quite important in kendo that when a point is struck the name of the specific point area must be called out in a very sharp voice at the time that contact is made with the point area. The only exception here is that the words *hidari* and *migi* are omitted when the name of the area is called out. This action of shouting the name of the area struck requires the kendo-ist to study each point opening continually, so that whenever practice is held he will easily and quickly call each point as he strikes or thrusts at the area with the *shinai.*

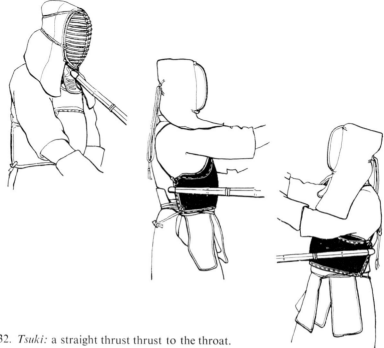

32. *Tsuki:* a straight thrust thrust to the throat.
33. *Migi-do:* a bold strike on the right side of the *do*.
34. *Hidari-do:* a similar stroke on the left of the *do*.

There is little need for strength in making a point. The forcefulness of each point comes with long hours of training in the hand position on the *shinai*.

Kendo match rules

The rules for the conduct of kendo matches, like those governing practice sessions in the *dojo* and those for the etiquette of kendo in general, are the result of centuries of development and refinement. They are given here in outline form.

 1. The officials will be as follows:
     a. A head judge, who will sit aside from the match.
     b. A forward judge in the contest area, to the right side.
     c. A forward judge in the contest area, to the left side.
     d. A rear judge in the contest area.
 2. There will also be the following technical personnel:
     a. A head timekeeper.

78

b. An official scorer.

c. Two line judges seated at opposite sides of the fencing area.

3. In judging the match, the following rules apply:

a. The forward judges will stand where both contestants are equally within their field of vision; will have authority over the general conduct of the match; will judge and rule on the validity of the cuts and thrusts; and will announce the results by extending the red or the white flag above the shoulder. If the point is not valid, the flags are rapidly crossed below the waist.

b. The rear judge has the same authority as the forward judge in judging and ruling on the validity of cuts and thrusts.

c. In cases where the decisions of the judges are not in agreement, they will consult with the head judge, and he will have the deciding vote.

d. The referee does not openly announce his opinion but makes it known to the forward judges in the contest area, who then announce the decision.

e. When the opinions of all three officials differ, the cut or thrust is held invalid.

4. After the contestants have bowed to each other, taken the *sonkyo* position, risen, and assumed the on-guard *maai* position, and after a brief moment to permit them to compose themselves, the forward judge will command: *"Hajime!"* (Commence!)

5. When one of the contestants gains a point, the forward judge will notice all of the flag positions and announce any one of the following points:

a. *Men.*

b. *Hidari-men.*

c. *Migi-men.*

d. *Kote.*

e. *Hidari-kote.*

f. *Hidari-do.*

g. *Migi-do.*

h. *Tsuki.*

6. At the announcement of a point, such as *"Men ari!"* (There is a *men* cut), the forward judge extends his flag to the right to indicate the scorer, and the contestants then return to their original in-center positions. The forward judge then announces: *"Nihomme"* (second point) or, when each contestant already has a point, *"Shobu"* (match point), and the bout continues. When the match has been decided, the forward judge announces:

79

"Shobu ari!" (There is a match point), and the bout is over.

7. When the forward judge indicates a decision, he does so by extending his arm with the flag fully above the shoulder.

8. When the forward judge interrupts the match because of an infraction of the rules or for some other reason, he calls: *"Yame!"* (Halt!), and when the call is made, he points in the direction of the contestant for whom time is called and to the timekeeper, who will raise a small red flag to denote time out. When the match is to be resumed, the forward judge calls: *"Hajime!"* and time is started.

9. When a contestant steps out of the match area, the foul-line flagman will raise either a red or a white flag, and the nearest judge will call: *"Yame! Moto no ichi ni kaere!"* (Halt! Return to your original position in the center!)

10. When the time limit of the match has expired (generally five minutes), the forward judge is warned by the head timekeeper, and the judge calls: *"Yame!"* The contestant with the point is then called the winner.

11. In cases of extensions of time, the forward judge announces: *"Encho"* (extension), and the contestants continue the match.

12. In group matches, the following rules apply:

a. According to a previously determined order, contestants will engage in a series of individual matches.

b. Group matches will be decided by one of two methods—either by total number of winners or by elimination, as follows:

(1) When the winning side is decided by the total number of winners, the group that has the greater number of victories wins. In the event of a tie, the tie is broken either by granting the decision to the group that scored the greater number of total points in the course of the matches or by allowing a representative from each group to engage in a match—in which case the winner's group gains the victory. It is a general rule that if the team captain does not win his match, then the team has lost.

(2) When the winning side is decided by the elimination method, the winners continue to engage winners from the opposing group until all but the last man is eliminated and the winning group is thus determined.

3

Fundamental Procedures and Techniques in Kendo

Practice preliminaries

The ancient formalities of the art of kendo are strictly adhered to in all phases of modern kendo. When the kendoists have assembled after the striking of the great drum, the captain of the *dojo* calls out: *"Ki o tsuke!"* (Sit up straight and pay attention!) As he inspects the *dojo,* he will notice that everyone is motionless, eyes to the front, hands properly in place. His second command will be *"Rei!"* (which is the command to bow), and all members will bow in the direction of the teacher or the head of the *dojo*.

The kendoist has put on his *tare* and *do* prior to entering the fencing area for the *rei* and has placed his *kote* together at his right, directly in front of his right knee. The *men,* with the flaps or wings extended and the *himo* placed inside, rests on top of the *kote* with its face piece down. If it is the regulation within the *dojo,* the *hachimaki* will be spread over the *men*.

The *shinai* is placed to the left with the *tsuba* in line with the left knee. The *hakama* is spread out and neatly tucked around the body. With this placement of the kendo equipment, the kendoist is ready to tie the *hachimaki* and the *men* in place and to fit his *kote* on each hand. As soon as the kendoist has tied his equipment properly and securely in place, he assumes the position shown in Fig. 27, which indicates that he will engage in practice. His protective armor is secure, and he has taken the *shinai* in his left hand, above the *tsuba*. The next procedure for the kendoist will be as

35–37. The *shizentai* (natural standing position).

follows: (1) he will stand and face the opposite side of the *dojo,* (2) bow to the head of the *dojo,* (3) notice any opponent who is ready, and (4) bow to this prospective opponent. The opponent will promptly return his bow, which is an invitation to practice. They will turn and face the head of the *dojo,* bow, turn again to each other, and, with a slight bow, walk directly into the fencing area.

As the kendoist walks to the fencing area, he takes the standing position known as *shizentai* (natural standing position) and shown in Figs. 35–37. This indicates that he is waiting to practice. The natural standing position finds him with his weight balanced on both feet and his arms hanging loosely at his sides, the left hand grasping the *shinai* above the *tsuba* and the *shinai* itself pointing backwards at a 45-degree slant. The beginner should bear in mind that the *shinai* represents a real sword, should be respected as such, and should be carried in this position. The kendoist always looks straight to the front and into the eyes of his opponent.

In the fencing area the kendoists take a position six paces apart and make a bow from the waist as a sign of recognition to opponent or teacher. During this bow the heels are together and the feet pointed outward in a 45-degree angle. The *shinai* is held firmly in a horizontal position (Fig. 38). After the bow the kendoists continue to face each other for a brief moment before taking the *sonkyo* position, which is a difficult crouching position.

82

38–39. The kendoists bow to each other and go into the *sonkyo* position before practice.

As they attain this position, the *shinai* is drawn as if from a scabbard, and the *sonkyo-kamae* position is taken.

Beginning position: Sonkyo

To begin the *sonkyo* position the kendoist, from the standing position, goes into a knee-bend with the *shinai* held at the side (Fig. 39). At the final moment of attaining the crouching position, the *shinai* is drawn, the right hand holding it just below the *tsuba* in the *tsuka* area. As the *shinai* is drawn slowly from the invisible scabbard, the left hand moves to the center of the body and grasps the *tsuka* at the very bottom, just as it comes into position with the sweeping movement of the right hand. The *shinai* is now

40. The *shinai* is drawn and held ready in the *sonkyo* position.

in the *kamae* or ready position, with the point in the direction of the opponent's chin or just in line with the *tsuki* (throat flap) of the *men* (Fig. 40). It is important to remember that each kendoist holds this crouching position without drawing the *shinai* until the senior or higher-ranking kendoist moves to the ready position by drawing his *shinai*. In a kendo match the *shinai* is drawn as the *sonkyo* position is reached.

Each *shinai*, still with its point or *kissaki* held in line with the opponent's eyes or between the chin and the *tsuki* of the *men,* crosses the other about three inches down from the *sakigawa* (Fig. 41). In this starting position the knees should be turned outward during the crouch. The weight of the body rests equally on the ball of each foot. The back is held straight, the head erect, and the chin up as the kendoist looks straight at his opponent. As shown in Fig. 41, the two kendoists are now ready to begin a practice bout *(keiko)* or a match *(shiai)*. It is important to understand that each kendoist holds this position until the senior or higher-ranking kendoist moves to the standing position. In a kendo match the position is held until the command to start is given by the *shimpan* or referee.

The kendoist shown in Fig. 40 has assumed the *sonkyo* position, drawn his *shinai,* and taken the *kamae* position to await the next movement. The front view given here clearly shows the cocked, relaxed position of the arms. The *hidari-kote* holds the *shinai* firmly in a pivot position directly in front of the body. The *migi-kote,* slightly on the relaxed side, holds the

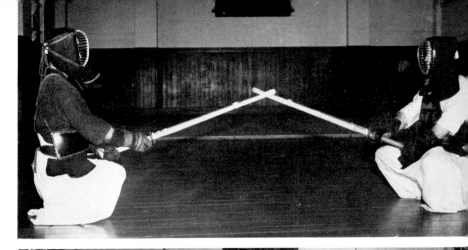

41–42. When the *shinai* are held ready, they cross close to the tips and are held in that position as the kendoists stand.

shinai just below the *tsuba*. The elbows are in close to the *do*. The back is straight, the head erect, and the eyes directly to the front.

In a match both kendoists rise at the referee's command to begin: *"Hajime!"* In a practice bout a mutual signal is enough. Both kendoists rise with the right foot pushed forward and the left drawn back slightly, while the *shinai* remain crossed (Fig. 42). The weight rests equally on both feet, and each *shinai* points directly at the opponent's eyes. There is thus less opportunity for the opponent to study the field as he looks for an opening to make his first move. The importance of holding the *shinai* directly in line with the opponent's eyes cannot be overstressed. The kendoist must gaze into his opponent's eyes and attempt to evaluate his every move. This is fundamental in the sport of kendo.

Even today in the most remote fencing halls in Japan or in foreign countries where kendo is practiced, this preliminary conduct is strictly adhered to by all kendoists. There is much more to this initial formality than mere discipline. It is the calmness and patience that are being taught to each fencer through each action that are important to understand.

Basic postures: kamae

Postures in holding the *shinai* vary according to kendo schools, but the following are common to all schools:

a. *chudan no kamae* or *chudan:* holding the *shinai* at the center of the body
b. *jodan no kamae* or *jodan:* holding the *shinai* over the head
c. *gedan no kamae* or *gedan:* holding the *shinai* low
d. *hasso no kamae* or *hasso:* holding the *shinai* vertically at right side of the head
e. *wakigamae:* holding the *shinai* at right side of the body with the *kissaki* pointing back

Musashi Miyamoto, one of the greatest swordsmen of the Tokugawa period, called these the Five Postures. Of the five, *chudan no kamae* is the most important and the most often used. It is a posture both for offense and defense. For example, when an opponent attacks, it serves as a defensive posture, but when he falls into an unguarded moment, he can be attacked from the same posture. The *jodan no kamae* is an offensive posture that requires a positively offensive spirit. The *gedan no kamae* is a defensive posture that requires mental preparation in the kendoist for converting his posture to an offensive one. The *kamae*, or ready positions for the *shinai* attack, are extremely important to master in kendo, for it is from these basic starting positions that all movements in kendo originate. In this book, however, only the first three are discussed.

The *chudan no kamae* (Fig. 43) is the basic form and must be mastered first. It is this position to which the kendoists return after each movement. In this *kamae* the *shinai* is held by grasping the *tsuka* firmly in the left hand, with the end of the *shinai* resting almost in the palm of the hand. The last

43. The *chudan no kamae* is the basic posture.

three fingers apply pressure, while the forefinger and thumb hold their position lightly. The thumb is pointing downward. With the left hand in place, the right hand takes a grip about one to two inches from the *tsuba,* with the last three fingers holding the *shinai* firmly and the forefinger and thumb relaxed. The thumb must be pointing downward.

The right foot is extended about 12 inches forward and the left foot about 12 inches to the left and drawn back an equal distance. The weight rests equally on each foot, and the heel of the left foot is raised about an inch and a half.

When holding the *shinai* in the palm of the hand and in the *chudan* position, it is important to remember that the tip is generally pointing at the opponent's *tsuki.* The *tsuki* flap is attached to the *men* and covers the throat. In holding the *men* in a semi-erect position, the throat area is protected by the flap, which touches the top of the *do.*

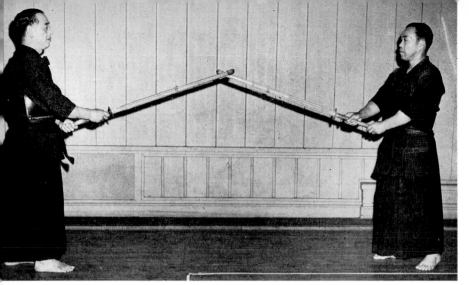

44-45. The *chudan no kamae:* demonstrated without armor and before warm-up exercises

The *chudan no kamae* is also shown in Figs. 44 and 45. In Fig. 44 the kendoists appear minus *men* and *kote*. Fig. 45 shows this basic starting position in a warm-up period at a *dojo*. One side defends, and the other attacks in the warming-up exercise called *kirikaeshi*. It should be noted in these illustrations that the *shinai* is held firmly in the left hand while the right grasps it in a light finger grip about two inches below the *tsuba*, as described above. There is always a space between the *tsuba* and the right hand. It should also be noted that the *shinai* cross at a point about three inches below the *sakigawa*. In this basic *chudan* position the back is straight,

46. The *jodan no kamae*.

47. The *gedan no kamae*.

the shoulders are drawn back, the head is erect, and the eyes look straight ahead.

The *jodan no kamae* (Fig. 46), in which the *shinai* is held over the head, calls for a body position in which the weight rests equally on both feet. The right foot is drawn back slightly, the heel raised an inch or two, while the left foot is slightly to the left and in front of the body. The *jodan no kamae* can be reversed: left foot drawn back and right foot extended, with hand positions also reversed. This *kamae* is discussed in greater detail later in this section.

Fig. 47 illustrates the *gedan no kamae* or dropping-the-guard posture. The *shinai* is grasped firmly in the left hand, while the right hand holds it lightly below the *tsuba*. The *shinai* is held with the point toward the opponent's right foot and about six inches above the floor.

48–50. Procedure for obtaining a correct grip on the *shinai.*

The hand grip for the shinai

The hand grip for the *shinai* is the first important technical step in kendo. The correct method of obtaining the grip with the left and the right hand on the *shinai,* together with the basic foot and arm positions that the beginning kendoist must practice, can be quickly achieved by following the directions outlined here.

The kendoist first takes the standing position with the right foot forward and the left foot drawn back. The *shinai* is grasped in the left hand, and the weight of the body rests equally on both feet (Fig. 48). After the student kendoist has mastered the hand and the finger position, the *kote* should be worn in order to get the actual feel of both *kote* and *shinai* (Fig. 51).

The left hand firmly grips the extreme end of the *shinai* and lowers the point or tip to the floor directly in front of and in line with the body. The feet have been kept in their basic position (Fig. 48). Therefore the tip of the *shinai* will be on a line centering the big toes. The *himo* or string running down the back of the *shinai* is always kept upward, since it is considered to represent the back of a real sword.

The kendoist continues to hold the *shinai* firmly in the palm of the left hand, the tip remaining in the initial position of contact with the floor. The right hand should then be raised above the head and allowed to fall slowly

51–55. The hand grip for the *shinai*.

in an arc toward the open space on the *shinai* between the *tsuba* and the left hand (Fig. 49). The right hand, after completing the downward arc, should rest on the *shinai* just an inch or so back of the *tsuba* and from three to five inches ahead of the thumb position of the left hand, which has retained its firm grip on the end of the *shinai* (Fig. 52).

The view of the *kamae* which is the basic form for holding the *shinai* (Fig. 50) illustrates one of the major points in kendo: that the left hand acts as the pivot and the right hand as the action lever of the *shinai*. The left hand draws the *shinai* in to the center of the body at a point just about one inch above the center flap of the *tare*. Generally the left hand should be held away from the body at a distance of about one closed fist.

The student kendoist should now raise the *shinai* and hold it in the basic starting position shown in Fig. 50, drawing his back into a straight position and raising his eyes to the front, with the head and shoulders square. He has now taken the solid ready-for-action position. The paramount rule in kendo is to have a feeling of being at ease but quite ready for action, without actual strain in holding the *shinai*.

The forefinger and thumb pressure of the right hand is actually applied in a resting manner along the top and side of the grip area of the *shinai*, as shown in Fig. 52. In the top view of the grip shown in Fig. 54 it should be noted that the right elbow is slightly cocked and the left arm poised in a relaxed position. The right hand is in line with the center of the kendoist's body. The bottom view of this position shown in Fig. 55 demonstrates how a complete circular movement is possible from the pivot formed by the *shinai* in a socket-like position, with the right arm ready to drive it in any direction.

The right-side view in Fig. 53 shows the extended position of the right arm and the pushing effect of the left arm. The movement of the left hand is almost expressing its basic pivot action. The student kendoist can quickly understand the hand grip if he compares it with the position and grasp of a baseball bat or a golf club, except that he pushes the left hand down to a level below the belt buckle and keeps the right arm and hand extended directly in front of his body.

The grip maintained on the *shinai* should be firm enough to withstand its being knocked entirely out of the hand, but it should give only slightly when struck. After being struck, the *shinai* should be quickly swung back into the ready-for-action position in case no opening has been found for the initial attack.

Force should not be used in kendo, for such action will only cause the kendoist to break or shatter the staves of his *shinai*. Moriji Mochida, who practices daily, generally will use the same *shinai* for a year without breaking one of the staves. This does not mean that Japan's 77-year-old top kendoist doesn't strike a resounding blow. In fact, the speed of Mochida's blow or thrust is sometimes quite bewildering, and the impact of his *shinai* is surprisingly forceful. However, it is the technique of delivering the blow—the wrist and finger control, the snap of the wrist, the body and leg movements combined—which accounts for the lightning movements of the master kendoist.

The kendoist must fully understand the correct feeling of the hand grip when he holds the *shinai* in the *suburi* movement described below. The beginning kendoist in Japan will often use a *hachimaki* or a small towel gripped in his hands to practice the relaxed yet firm *suburi* hand movement. The student kendoist should think of the grip as similar to that of taking a wet towel in his hands and wringing out the water. He should begin with his *shinai* in the ready position and go through the *suburi* movements, concentrating on bringing the *shinai* through all of the movements with this feeling of the wringing motion in each forward stroke. The hands should almost be opened in their relaxed position above the head. As the *shinai* is brought down to the ready position, the hands become tight and end in a firm, but not strained, grip, using a whiplike movement to bring the *shinai* rapidly down into this position.

This downward movement of the hands holding the *shinai* produces the effect of squeezing a towel—the left hand rotating towards the right hand and the right hand moving in a rotating manner towards the left, both thumbs pointing ahead and downward at the end of their inward rotation. These movements should always be fully executed in the *suburi* sequence and followed in future periods of training so that they will become second nature to the kendoist.

93

The footwork and the movement of the shinai: suburi

In kendo there is this saying: "The eyes first, the footwork next, the courage third, and the strength fourth." In other words, the footwork is valued next to the sight. People are apt to think that in kendo those sportsmen who are muscular and courageous must have the advantage over those who are not. In fact, however, this is not so. Of course these two factors are quite necessary, but what is required first of all is keenness of sight and insight to observe the opponent's posture and detect any unpreparedness in him. Next, it is essential for the kendoist to possess a skill in footwork that will enable him to approach his opponent and attack him as quickly as lightning. Since old times it has even been said: "In order to learn the techniques, exercise your footwork first rather than your handwork."

The footwork in kendo must be mastered simultaneously with the arm movements. They should be as one in the kendoist's action. Fig. 56 illustrates the basic movement called *suburi*. This is the movement of the *shinai* in a series of motions back over the head, each motion simulating a point —*kote, men,* or *do.* The arm motions are accompanied by a forward or backward sliding movement of the feet.

In Fig. 56*a* the kendoist is shown in the ready position. The right foot is forward, the left foot drawn back with the heel raised about four inches and the knee slightly bent. Hips are level; the back is straight; and the shoulders are back and square. The arms are in a cocked position, with the left hand at the center of the body and the right hand held just above and directly to the front in a relaxed position. The *shinai* is grasped tightly at the end by the left hand, while the right hand cradles the area near the *tsuba.*

The first movement is shown in *b:* a sliding motion forward with the right foot, which must be kept along the same plane as the floor. At the same time the arms are extended and the *shinai* begins its movement up over the head *(c, d, e).* The left foot slides slowly up to a position under the left hip.

At the crown of the head *(e)* the arms are unlocked so that the *shinai* will feel comfortable as it is grasped with the hands over the head, which is its position prior to its backward motion. In *f* the kendoist moves for-

56. *Suburi,* the basic practice exercise.

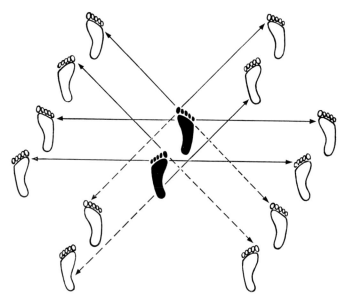

57. The pattern of kendo footwork.

ward and allows the *shinai* to fall behind him with arms bent. This movement has a shoulder-relaxing factor and is an excellent exercise for conditioning the back and shoulder muscles. As the arm movement is made, the right foot has been extended. The left foot is propelling the body forward, and it remains slightly to the rear, with the heel raised about two inches.

The forward movement is a reversal of this sequence, with the arms coming from the raised, locked position and bringing the *shinai* downward with a cutting movement as the right foot slides forward and the left leg propels the body forward. The body is still held straight, with the head back and the chin tucked in. It is important to remember not to tighten the shoulders in this exercise. The arms must be relaxed.

The position of the feet (Fig. 56) must be understood prior to the *suburi* exercise. The feet are separated by about the length of one foot. The right foot is firmly planted on the sole, with the heel slightly raised. The left foot is drawn back to the rear so that the toe is just in line with the heel of the right foot and about a foot length away to the left.

Fig. 57 shows the footwork for the various movements in kendo. This footwork must be mastered, and the best approach is constant practice. Starting from the shaded position, the kendoist moves to the left with his left foot first and to the right with his right foot first. The square or box movement can be accomplished by first moving the right foot to the right, followed by the left foot. Then move the left foot back and follow the movement with the right foot. The next movement will be to the left with the left foot, the right foot following. To complete the box, the right foot is pushed forward, and the left foot follows. The *shinai* can be moved in a *suburi* movement: *hidari-men, men, migi-men,* then *men.*

The *shinai* must be swung along a strictly proper course and not at random. If the kendoist has learned the proper course, he will be able to swing even a very heavy *shinai* with only two fingers of each hand. If he does not know the proper course, however, he will have to throw too much strength into his arms and will still be unable to swing the *shinai* swiftly and strongly.

Suburi is a good exercise for making the movement of the *shinai* coincide with that of the body. It is useful also as a preparatory and supplementary exercise for kendo practice. Through it the kendoist can train and strengthen the muscles needed for kendo, such as those of the upper and lower limbs. In performing *suburi* the kendoist must not swing the *shinai* very swiftly from the beginning but must swing it openly, mildly, and properly. With further practice, he will become able to swing it more strongly and swiftly.

Basic strokes

There are many *waza* or techniques in kendo, but all of these come from the basic strokes: *men* (top front of the mask), *migi-men* (right side of the mask), *hidari-men* (left side of the mask), *kote* (right forearm), *hidari-kote* (left forearm), *migi-do* (right side of the chest protector), *hidari-do* (left side of the chest protector), and *tsuki* (throat flap).

Having been taught these basic strokes, the beginning kendoist practices them by beating the air. He imagines that he has an opponent in the space before him. At the start, he practices swinging the *shinai* slowly and correctly and later by swinging it more swiftly and strongly. When he becomes good at it, his *shinai* strokes will make a whirring sound as they cut the air. But if he does not swing the *shinai* properly, his strokes will make no sound, no matter how swiftly or strongly he swings it.

Next the kendoist tries his strokes on a knocking stick or a knocking base. By striking such real objects he learns well how to snap his wrists and set his palms and fingers around the *tsuba*. He also learns that if he does not set his palms and his wrists tightly yet flexibly, he cannot consistently hit the target at the proper point.

97

At last the kendoist practices with his teacher, a junior kendoist, or a friend. The two face each other and practice striking the various points. Since the target is now a moving one, he is not able to hit each point until he becomes accustomed to the situation. But when his strike is successful, he has the same exhilaration as that of hitting a home run in a baseball game.

Basic strokes are the most important things in kendo, and the kendoist must practice them patiently under the guidance of his teachers. If he abandons this practice at the halfway mark and hastily begins free practice or engages in a match, he cannot master proper posture or guard, and his *waza* (techniques) will be faulty. No kendoist can afford to neglect the practice of the basic strokes.

98

58–59. Making the *kote* point. The left hand is always held directly in front, acting as pivot.

Making the kote point

Perhaps the most frequently used point in kendo is the *kote* point. To make this point as illustrated in Fig. 58, a blow is delivered to the forearm of the right *kote*. The left *kote* is never struck in a fencing match, bout, or practice session except when the *shinai* is held above the *do* in the *jodan* position.

In Fig. 59 the kendoist has made a half sidestep to the left, bringing his *shinai* down so that the right arm is in a semicocked position. The left hand is directly in front of the kendoist, acting as a pivot for this movement. The left foot is back, with the heel raised, and the weight rests equally on both feet. The kendoist continues to look directly into the eyes of his opponent to ascertain the next movement. As the blow is made, the kendoist must simultaneously cry out *"Kote!"* Of course, if there is another opening, the contest continues, and the next point is attempted.

60–61. Approach and delivery of the *men* attack.

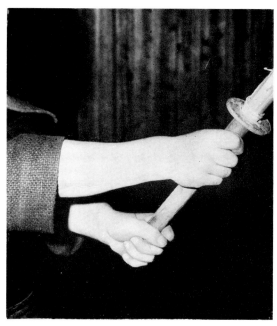

62. The proper grip for
the *men* attack.

The men attack and the footwork

In Fig. 60 the kendoist on the left is making the *men* approach with the *shinai* raised, the right arm stretched in axis with the body, and the left arm drawn to the center of the body. (The left *kote* seldom leaves the center of the body.) In the forward movement the kendoist must make his jump with dispatch.

When the attack reaches the final point, the *shinai* will be brought down directly on the top center of the opponent's *men* (Fig. 61). The right leg has stepped out into a lunging position with the sole and heel flat on the floor, the left foot acting as a brake on the forward movement. Notice also in Fig. 61 that the *hakama,* because it is divided, does not bind any leg movement. As the attack is made, the blow to the head must be struck simultaneously with the shout of *"Men!"*—that is, the point being made.

Fig. 62 shows the proper manner of gripping the *shinai* in making the *men* attack. The right hand grasps it at a distance of two fingers below the *tsuba* with a firm but light grip. With the end of the *shinai* resting on its palm, the left hand grasps it in a pivot grip, holding the *shinai* directly at the center of the body. The thumbs are always pointed downward about 45 degrees. The forefinger and thumb of the left hand grasp the *shinai* while the other three fingers act as a pivot in gripping it. This pivot grip of the left hand is used in every movement of kendo. The right arm is extended directly in front and in the same plane as that of the body.

101

63–64. Two variations of the *yokomen* attack.

The yokomen attack

Normally a surprise attack, the *yokomen* or side-*men* blow may be made with either hand. The movement begins from the *chudan, gedan,* or *jodan* position. Gripping the *shinai* in either the right or the left hand, the kendoist makes a half circle to the right or to the left, depending on which hand holds the *shinai*.

102

In the left-handed attack shown in Fig. 63 the left foot pushes forward and steps about five degrees to the left, while the right foot is stretched and planted firmly in position on the *dojo* floor. As the attack is made, the kendoist calls out: *"Yokomen!"*

To carry out the left-handed *yokomen* attack shown in Fig. 64, the right elbow is drawn as far back as possible so that the *kote* is in line with the *do*. The *shinai* is grasped firmly at the end and in the center of the grip area of the *kote*. Note that the left foot is extended well forward. The knees are slightly bent, hips are level, the waist is straight, shoulders are drawn back, and the head is erect. As the kendoist strikes the blow, he shouts: *"Yokomen!"*

The do attack

Figs. 65 and 66 show the blow for the chest protector called *do*. This blow is delivered to either side of the opponent's *do*. A rapid forward movement is necessary in the *do* attack, which is made from either a standing or a moving position, backward or forward. In Fig. 65 the kendoist on the right has moved forward with his right foot and has brought himself in range so that he can strike the right side of his opponent's *do*. In Fig. 66 the kendoist on the left has made a rapid lunge forward to evade his opponent's intended *men* attack. It is of interest to note the position of the attacker's hands in these two figures, which show that the right hand has crossed over to the left side. The left hand continues to be at the center of the body, but it pushes the *shinai* to the right. While this crossing of the hands is not characteristic of every type of *do* attack, it is frequently required for success-ful delivery of the blow.

Fig. 67 shows a close-up of the position of the hands on the *shinai* in a crossover type of *do* attack. The *shinai* is held in a natural grip, with the left hand firmly grasping the end and the right in a semitight hold. The forward movement of the right hand in a rolling-over motion places the thumb at a nine-o'clock position. The hand position is used as an axis for the blow and must remain at the center of the attacker's body. As the *shinai* makes its contact, the attacker must call his point: *"Do!"*

The sequence comprising Figs. 68–70 shows the development of a *do*

65–66. Two variations of the *do* attack.

67. The proper grip for the cross-over *do* attack.

attack. In Fig. 68 the kendoists are in the ready position waiting for the first move. In Fig. 69 the opponent on the left has raised his *shinai* into the *jodan* position, and the kendoist on the right, seeing the chance for a *do* strike, has moved forward to take advantage of it. His left foot, followed by the right, has started the forward movement simultaneously with the dropping of the *shinai*.

The element of surprise in the *do* attack can be understood because of the comparatively great distance that must be covered in a fraction of a

68–70. Development of the *do* attack: the ready position, the opening (the kendoist on the left exposes his *do* by going into the *jodan* position), and the attack.

105

71–72. Two variations of the *tsuki* thrust.

second. In Fig. 70 the kendoist has completed the long stride forward and delivered his blow, making a successful *migi-do* attack by going to his left and underneath his opponent's projected *men* attack. The *shinai* has crossed in front and well to the left while carrying the blow forward to the opponent. This draws the opponent to the attacker, and as he advances, the attacker parries and cuts underneath to make the *do* point. The opponent's forward movement may be utilized in this particular technique. Simultaneously with the making of the point the attacker must call out: *"Do!"*

106

The tsuki thrust

The only thrust in kendo is *tsuki,* the lunge at the throat. This attack, shown in Fig. 71, requires a slight forward motion of the body at great speed. The arms are extended directly in front of the kendoist but not above the axis of the shoulders. In the two-handed lunge shown in this figure, the *shinai* is thrust out to the opponent's throat with the *sakigawa* aimed at the vicinity of the padded throat flap under the chin of the *men.* This padded flap acts as a protection against this thrust, and there is another flap under it to serve as additional protection. As the kendoist makes his point, he simultaneously calls out: *"Tsuki!"*

The *tsuki* thrust may be made with both hands or with the right or the left hand only. The hand position for the two-handed *tsuki* thrust is in the form of a hugging of the *shinai* with the right arm straight and the left arm in a semicocked position.

The left-hand thrust is illustrated in Fig. 72. The position of the *sakigawa* or tip of the *shinai* must be directly in front of the opponent's *men* and aimed at the protecting throat flap. The elbows are locked in the forward movement. The position of the right leg is forward. The knees are slightly bent; the left foot is arched; and the weight rests equally on the toes. The hips are drawn back; the torso is straight; the shoulders are level; and the head is erect. As the thrust is made, the kendoist shouts: *"Tsuki!"* The attacker must be prepared for the opponent's counterattack because of the openings that the *tsuki* attack permits. The *tsuki* attack described here may also be carried out with the right hand.

Repetition of strokes: kirikaeshi

Kirikaeshi, the repetition of strokes, is the best way for the kendoist to exercise collectively the basic actions that he has learned. Years ago it was commonly said that the beginner required three years' practice in *kirikaeshi,* and kendo instructors would compel beginners to undergo such training for a long time. With the progress of methods in kendo guidance today, practice of this kind is not given continuously for such a long period. On

107

the other hand, it is necessary for the kendoist to undertake this basic training occasionally, even if he has improved his kendo art.

In *kirikaeshi* the kendoist practices first as attacker and then as receiver, changing places with his opponent and reversing the roles. As attacker, he first assumes the *chudan no kamae* and delivers a *men* strike. Then, he strikes the opponent's left and right *men* from right and then from left by turns. This is repeated several times. Next, he takes a step backward, assumes a *chudan* posture, and strikes the front of the *men* once to start another course of *kirikaeshi*.

He repeats the same course again and again until he becomes exhausted both physically and mentally. Then he strikes the opponent's front *men*. While he is vigorous, the kendoist is apt to depend so much on his physical and mental strength that he will be unable to strike the opponent's front *men* properly. But when he has spent his physical and mental strength in the *kirikaeshi* practice, he will really know how to deliver the front *men* blow properly.

In playing the role of receiver, when the opponent strikes his front *men* the kendoist allows him to strike it properly to the point. Then, when the opponent successively delivers strokes to the left and right *men* by turns, he receives each strike with his *shinai* by holding it straight up before him in such a manner as to draw the opponent's strokes toward him while stepping back. When the opponent steps back to continue his *kirikaeshi,* the receiver steps forward to receive the left and right strokes by turns in the same manner. Then, when the opponent assumes a *chudan* posture, the receiver will also assume the same posture to let him strike the front *men*. As receiver, the kendoist must be careful to create an adequate interval at which the attacker can strike him easily and at the proper time.

There is an old kendo proverb: "The *kirikaeshi* gives ten virtues to the attacker and eight virtues to the receiver." The ten virtues for the attacker are that *kirikaeshi* (1) makes his *waza* sharp and swift, (2) strengthens the power of his stroke, (3) gives him good wind and stamina, (4) makes the working of his arms flexible, (5) makes his physical movement light and agile, (6) enables him to operate the *shinai* freely, (7) settles his waist well and gives him a well-balanced posture, (8) makes his eyesight clear, (9) teaches him the adequate interval at which to strike his opponent, and

(10) gives him dexterity in the working of his palms. The eight virtues for the receiver are that *kirikaeshi* (1) keeps his mind in tranquillity, (2) makes his eyesight clear, (3) makes him learn the style of his opponent's sword-stroke techniques, (4) makes his palms firm and flexible, (5) makes his physical movement free and flexible, (6) enables him to become good at receiving strikes, (7) strengthens his arms, and (8) strengthens his body.

Making a point from the jodan position

Whenever the kendoist takes the *jodan* position, with arms and *shinai* raised above the head as shown in Fig. 73, any one of the points can be scored, provided the attacker can skillfully evade offensive action or a defense against his attack. To make a move from the *jodan* position for *men, kote, do, tsuki,* or any combination, the following points must be observed. The body should be straight, not twisted or tilted. The left foot is in front, the right almost to the extreme rear, well in and under the body. The weight rests equally on both feet but tends to favor the right foot. The kendoist should face his opponent directly, using a light grip on the *shinai,* the left hand gripping the end of the *tsuka* with force. The elbows should be in a cocked position, with the hands above the head. From this position the kendoist considers the point openings available to him. The position can be reversed: left foot drawn back and right foot extended, with hand positions also reversed.

In Fig. 74 the kendoist on the left has raised his *shinai* above his head in the *jodan no kamae* while his opponent defends in a "high" *chudan no kamae* with his *shinai* raised in anticipation of the attack. For the *jodan* position the left arm should be drawn in and close to the *men,* with the left hand just above the left shoulder. The right hand is raised so that the elbow is above the right ear and the *kote* is drawn close to the top of the *men.* The blow from the *jodan* position is made by a throwing-descending motion of the *shinai* toward the opponent's *kote* or *men.* To make the throwing-descending motion with the *shinai,* the kendoist should have the feeling of throwing the *shinai,* with the left hand guiding the downward movement.

When making the move for a point, the kendoist must carry out the movement with dispatch. He should have the feeling that he is throwing

109

73. The *jodan* position.

74. The *jodan* position is countered by a slightly raised *chudan* position.

the *shinai* forward to the opponent. It is the whip-throwing manner that gives the *shinai* the speed to avoid any defense that the opponent may contrive. The *shinai* should never be lower than the opponent's *men* after the blow has been struck. If at the *kote*, the blow should not be below the *tare*.

The timing is vital in the movement from the *jodan* position. The *shinai* should be held very steady, since the opponent will move about for an advantage. The right hand is held above the head and to the rear, acting as a cradle for the *shinai*. The cradling position affords the kendoist a propelling force in shoving the *shinai* forward as it is accelerated by the left arm in the throwing-descending movement. The left hand should not grip the *shinai* too firmly but should allow freedom of movement. The right foot moves in a sidestep, with the left foot striking off to the left, swinging the body around halfway to the right of the opponent.

Tsuba-zeriai: the close-contact shinai

Fig. 75 shows the kendoists in the close fencing position called *tsuba-zeriai*. In this position the *shinai* are crossed in a vertical position, and the *tsuba* is held close to the opponent's *shinai*. The right *kote* is moved very close to the *tsuba*. Each kendoist is using the left hand as a solid axis for his future movement in parrying the opponent's *shinai*, which must not touch the body at any area in this position. It should be noted that the body is vertical, the weight resting equally on both feet and the feet drawn close together. Each kendoist is trying to raise his opponent's *shinai* with his *tsuba* so that he can either step back and make the blow for *kote, men,* or *do,* or the thrust for *tsuki*.

The aiuchi point

In Fig. 76 the kendoist on the left has made a two-handed *hidari-men* attack—that is, an attack on the left side of the opponent's *men*. At the same time the kendoist on the right has countered with a left-side two-handed *do* attack. Both points are good. The judge would call the action a draw: *"Aiuchi, hidari-men, hidari-do."* Neither kendoist would score a point, since each struck his respective point at the same time *(aiuchi)*. The match would continue.

111

75. The *tsuba-zeriai,* the close contact *shinai.*

76. The *aiuchi* point: the contestants each make a point at the same time. They cancel each other, and neither is counted.

77. The *nito* or two-*shinai* attack.

Nito: the two-shinai attack

Fig. 77 illustrates the *nito* or two-*shinai* attack. The *nito* kendoist, with a short *shinai* in his left hand and a lighter three-quarter-length *shinai* in his right hand, faces his opponent, who has a regulation-length *shinai* held in a semi-*gedan no kamae*—that is, a position slightly lower than normal. This is one of the best defensive actions in *nito*. The short *shinai* of the attacker is used as a parrying weapon or shield and is held even with the tip of the opponent's *shinai* in a horizontal position. The three-quarter-length *shinai* is raised in a *jodan* position above the head.

The front view of the *nito* attack in Fig. 78 shows the parrying position of the short *shinai* in the defense against a *men* attack. The right hand is holding the three-quarter-length *shinai* with the elbow slightly lower than in the two-handed, above-the-head *migi-jodan* position. The left arm is held in front with the hand gripping the short *shinai* in a ready position. The point of the *shinai* is held in line with the opponent's *tsuki*. The right foot is planted well forward, the knee slightly bent. The left foot, with the heel raised about two inches, is to the rear and in a driving position. The right hand is raised with the three-quarter-length *shinai* poised for a *men* or a *kote* attack.

113

78. Frontal view of the *nito* attack.

79. Making the *hidari-kote* point in a *nito* attack.

The hidari-kote point in the nito attack

In Fig. 79 the *nito* kendoist in the white *keikogi* and *hakama* has made a *nito* attack on the left *kote* of the opponent in black. When the opponent is in the *jodan* position, with both hands raised above the head (as shown in the figure), either *kote* is vulnerable, as well as the *tsuki, do,* or *men.* In making his *nito* attack, the kendoist has his right foot extended forward, pushing off with his left foot. The short *shinai* is held above the top of the *men* as a shield in the defensive position against the downward movement of the opponent's *shinai* from the *jodan* position.

114

80. Making the *men* point in a *nito* attack.

The men attack against the jodan position

In Fig. 80 the kendoist in white has drawn in close to his opponent for a *men* attack. The three-quarter-length *shinai* has been aimed at the *men* of the defender in black. The attacker's right foot is extended, with the knee bent, and the body has pushed forward in a movement propelled by the left foot, the heel of which is lifted off the *dojo* floor. The hand holding the short *shinai* is held in a defensive position to ward off any blow coming from the defender's *jodan* position.

115

81. At the close of a bout the kendoists bow to each other.

82. Post-practice instructions.

The close of the practice period

As in the ancient past, the beating of the *taiko* or great drum calls the kendo practice period to a close. The drawn-out cry of *"Yame-e-e-e!"* by the *dojo* captain signifies that the practice period is over for the day. With this announcement, the kendoists assume the *sonkyo-kamae* position, returning the *shinai* to its imaginary sheath. They rise facing each other, withdraw three steps backward, and bow again. If the kendoist is very pleased with the practice, he extends his right hand downward at a 45-degree angle and bows again to his opponent. (Fig. 81). They stand for a

116

83. A student shows respect to his teacher. The teacher here is Moriji Mochida, 10th *dan, hanshi,* the highest ranking kendo teacher in Japan.

moment and then retire from the fencing area, returning to their assigned positions in the *dojo.*

Generally the kendoist will keep his *men* firmly secured until the end of the practice. During his rest period the equipment should be retied or straightened. When the kendoist returns to his assigned position in the *dojo,* he will take off his *kote* and place them at his right with the *men* on top. The *hachimaki* will then be spread out over the top of the *men* to dry. The *shinai* is always placed on the left side, with the grip to the front and the *tsuba* in line with the left knee. The kendoist is then ready to listen to post-practice critiques or instructions (Fig. 82).

At the command of *"Rei!"* (which is the signal to bow), the kendoists will bow to each other in recognition of the completion of a practice period. (Fig. 81). Following this formality, the lower-ranking kendoists will place themselves before each teacher and, in a kneeling position (Fig. 83), thank him for the practice and his instructions with a low bow. This etiquette is also carried out toward each opponent with whom he has practiced during the period. It is a custom that has been practiced in the *dojo* for more than one thousand years, and it is considered highly essential to the mental and moral training of the kendoist, who is required to respect his opponent at all times. This is part of the kendo tradition, and it survives to this day as an aspect of the discipline in a *dojo* training period. It has become a symbol of sportsmanship and good manners as well as a display of humble respect.

117

4

Offensive and Receiving Techniques

Application

In kendo, application means a technique *(waza)* for applying the various basic strokes (strikes and thrusts) and actions in a practice session or a match between two kendoists. As a rule, the applied actions are carried out with an opponent. A *waza* that can be exercised without an opponent is a basic action and not an applied one. Among applied techniques there are two kinds: *shikake-waza* or offensive techniques and *oji-waza* or receiving techniques.

Shikake-waza

Shikake-waza are techniques of giving a stroke by taking advantage of the opponent's being off guard. It is necessary for beginners in kendo to exercise these techniques well. In kendo, to forestall the opponent is most important, and the beginner must cultivate the spirit of doing things positively by learning the *shikake-waza* thoroughly. There are many kinds of *shikake-waza: harai-waza* (warding-off technique), *nidan-* or *sandan-waza* (two- or three-step technique), *debana-waza* (attacking-at-the-start technique), *katsugi-waza* (shouldering-the-sword technique), *hiki-waza* (stepping-back technique), *katate-waza* (single-hand technique), and *jodan-waza* (technique of holding the sword over the head).

119

84. *Harai-men:* the opponent's *shinai* is warded off as the *men* attack is executed.

1. HARAI-WAZA

The human being performs a natural action in trying to ward off obstacles that appear before him. In kendo also, an opponent can be beaten aside if there is no obstacle about him. If, however, he holds a *shinai* in his hand, aiming it at his partner, the partner cannot freely give him a stroke. If the partner forcibly tries to beat off such an opponent, he may be struck by a contrary force or at least checked. It is therefore necessary for the kendoist first to ward off his opponent's *shinai* by delivering a stroke and thus unbalancing his posture so that the kendoist can make a *men, kote,* or *do* strike or a *tsuki* thrust. This is called *harai-waza,* a technique that is divided into *harai-men, harai-kote, harai-do,* and *harai-tsuki,* according to the target region.

In any of these instances, however, the kendoist must not ward off his opponent's *shinai* transversely. If he makes such a horizontal movement,

120

85–86. *Harai-kote:* an oblique blow first wards off the opponent's *shinai* before the *kote* is attacked.

he will have to swing his *shinai* over his head again and then swing it down toward the target—a two-step action that delays the stroke. Worse still, the kendoist may be struck while he is on the way toward starting another action. The proper course, therefore, is for the kendoist to swing his *shinai* in such a way as to ward off the opponent's *shinai* as his own swings upward. Only *harai-men* and *harai-kote* will be discussed here.

    a. *Harai-men* (Fig. 84)

    The kendoist and his opponent face each other. Discovering his opponent off guard, the kendoist steps forward with his right foot, wards off his opponent's *shinai* in a right-upward direction with the left side of his own *shinai,* swings his *shinai* overhead, and, at the same time, draws his left foot up beside his right foot and delivers a blow on the opponent's front *men.* In this case, the kendoist must skillfully snap his wrists upward in a small and yet keen action to ward off the opponent's *shinai* in an upward direc-

87. The *kote-men* combination.   88. The *kote-do* combination.

tion. If he wishes to ward off the opponent's *shinai* in an upward direction on the opposite side, he can do so by the same method.

b. *Harai-kote* (Figs. 85-86)

This is a smaller *waza* than the *harai-men,* but the manner of carrying it out is nearly the same. The kendoist first wards off the opponent's *shinai* with a slight oblique movement upward and to the right and then strikes his right *kote*. If the stroke to the *kote* is not complete, however, the opponent will in most cases make a dodge or a counterattack. Therefore the kendoist must remember to make the stroke resolutely.

2. NIDAN- OR SANDAN-WAZA

This is a technique by which the kendoist continuously attacks a second and/or a third target as soon as he finds that his first stroke has been unsuccessful. In this case he must not attack in an easygoing way but must deliver each stroke with all his might. This *waza* offers two courses: to attack the *kote* first and then attack some other target or to attack either the *men* or the *tsuki* first and then another target. The three fundamental instances of *kote-men, kote-do,* and *men-do* will be presented here.

89. The *men-do* combination.

a. *Kote-men* (Fig. 87)

The kendoist and his opponent face each other in the *chudan* position. Catching the opponent in an unguarded moment, the kendoist attacks his right *kote*, upon which the opponent defends his right *kote* by stepping back and lowering his *shinai*. Taking advantage of this chance, the kendoist immediately delivers a front-*men* blow.

b. *Kote-do* (Fig. 88)

The kendoist and his opponent face each other in the *chudan* position. Catching the opponent in an unguarded moment, the kendoist attacks his right *kote*, upon which he lifts his hands (unlike the case in *kote-men*) and leaves his *do* open to attack in his attempt to dodge. Keenly seizing this opportunity, the kendoist steps forward obliquely to the right and delivers a blow to the right *do*.

c. *Men-do* (Fig. 89)

The kendoist and his opponent are watching for a chance while maintaining the *chudan* posture. The kendoist steps resolutely in, aiming at the opponent's *men*, upon which the opponent unintentionally lifts his hands in an attempt to defend his *men* or slidingly ward off the kendoist's *shinai* but at the same time leaves his right *do* open to attack. Without missing

123

this chance, the kendoist steps forward obliquely to the right and delivers a blow to the right *do*.

These are the essentials of the *nidan-* and *sandan-waza*. The *sandan-waza* can be carried out easily if the kendoist only combines the two techniques of *kote-men* and *men-do*. What he must be careful about in performing this technique is to give a resolute stroke at the first attack and to drive on to the next attack without stopping. In other words, it is important for him not to stop his action halfway.

3. DEBANA-WAZA

This is a technique for delivering a stroke immediately without missing an opportunity when the opponent lifts his hands in an attempt to start an attack or just when he is starting his motion to advance. Three instances offer the best chances of attack: when the opponent has just finished an action, when the posture of his body has settled down, and when he is just on the verge of starting an action. In this sense the kendoist must keep a careful watch upon his opponent, maintaining a keen mind in order not to miss even the slightest sign of the start of his opponent's action and, at the same time, must maintain a resolute mind in order to put himself into action as soon as he catches the opponent in an unguarded moment. The *debana-waza* consist of *debana-men*, *debana-kote*, and *debana-tsuki*. Of these, only the first two are explained here.

a. *Debana-men*

The kendoist and his opponent face each other in the *chudan* posture. The technique of *debana-men* calls for the kendoist to resolutely deliver a front-*men* blow to the opponent just when he moves his body slightly forward and the point of his *shinai* stirs as he attempts a blow. Since this stroke involves taking advantage of an important chance, it is necessary for the kendoist to refrain from making too big a swing with his *shinai*, to dash in well, and to deliver a resolute blow as at the risk of his life.

b. *Debana-kote*

The kendoist and his opponent face each other in the *chudan* posture. Just when the opponent lifts his hands in an attempt to deliver a *men* blow, the kendoist seizes the opportunity to hit his right *kote* with a contrary

124

90–91. The *hiki-men:* a *men* attack is delivered while withdrawing from a scuffle at close quarters *(tsuba-zeriai)*.

force. The technique is almost the same as that of *debana-men,* except that the *debana-kote* requires a small and yet sharp stroke.

4. HIKI-WAZA

This is a technique to be employed in the case when the kendoist and his opponent are pushing against each other's *shinai* guard *(tsuka-gashira)*. In such a case the kendoist is likely to be so close to his opponent that he cannot put enough strength into his stroke. Accordingly, he must study the chances and the possible movements of his body in order to deliver an accurate stroke.

a. *Hiki-men* (Figs. 90–91)

While the kendoist and his opponent are pushing each other's *shinai* guard, the kendoist finds a chance to step back, and the opponent, affected by this move, steps forward, stretches his hands, and so exposes an unguarded point on his front *men*. Without a moment's delay the kendoist swings his *shinai* overhead and delivers a *men* blow. In order to do an effective job of making the opponent unintentionally drop his guard, the kendoist may just push his *kote* region. If he is affected by such an attempt and pushes back, the kendoist can seize this good chance. In order to master this technique it is important for the kendoist to study various ways of getting his opponent off guard.

b. *Hiki-kote*

While the kendoist and his opponent are pushing each other's *shinai* guard, the kendoist slightly pushes the opponent's *kote* region obliquely right forward. If the opponent is affected by this and unintentionally pushes back, consequently stretching his arms, the kendoist then takes a step back obliquely left and strikes the opponent's right *kote*. In such a case, if the opponent's arms are lifted, it will be all the more convenient for the stroke. It may therefore be good for the kendoist to try pushing the opponent's left fist upward with his own left fist in order to create a chance. There is, however, one thing about which the kendoist must be very careful: when he is going to drive his *shinai* to the other side of his opponent's *shinai*, he must not hold his *shinai* too far from him and must always keep his palms soft and relaxed.

c. *Hiki-do*

While the kendoist and his opponent are pushing each other's *shinai* guard, the kendoist takes a step backwards and swings his *shinai* up overhead. Affected by this move, the opponent lifts his hands, and the kendoist instantly strikes his *do*. In this case, too, it is an important condition that the opponent's arms be lifted. For this purpose, it may be good for the kendoist to push the opponent's *kote* region downward and then make use of the reaction in which his arms are consequently lifted—or to attempt to push up the opponent's left fist with his own left fist. The kendoist can also perform the *hiki-do* by striking the opponent's *do* upon stepping forward with his left foot and backward with his right. In any case it is very important for the kendoist to turn his hands well in striking the opponent's *do,* and for this reason he must always keep his palms soft and relaxed and at the same time make use of the strength of his twisted waist when performing this technique.

5. KATSUGI-WAZA

This technique is advantageous when using a comparatively long *shinai.* In kendo schools of the days when warriors wore armor and long swords, they used to swing their swords up across the left shoulder and then down to attack the enemy. In modern kendo, of course, fencers do not wear this type of armor. Still, if the kendoist resolutely shoulders his *shinai* at a distant interval from his opponent, the opponent, affected by such a move, may lift or lower his arms, and the kendoist may find a good chance to attack.

Accordingly, the *katsugi-waza* is a kind of enticing technique and quite an advantageous one. On the other hand, the kendoist may be struck by the opponent in case he shoulders his *shinai* in an incomplete way or is at too close an interval with the opponent. It is important to be careful about this. This *waza* is divided into *katsugi-men, katsugi-kote,* and *katsugi-do,* but since all of these are advanced techniques, they will not be discussed here.

6. JODAN-WAZA

This technique calls for holding the *shinai* above the head in a *jodan* posture and then swinging it down upon the opponent with great resolution just when he is about to advance or retreat. The *jodan no kamae* is a very strong posture, as has been noted earlier in this book. Once the kendoist has determined to use the *jodan-waza,* it is essential that he have an extremely strong fighting spirit toward his opponent. Since this technique cannot be learned in the early stages of kendo training, an explanation of it is omitted here.

92. *Katate-waza:* single-handed, long-range attack.

7. KATATE-WAZA (Fig. 92)

This single-hand technique can be likened to a missile. It is a technique designed to enable the kendoist to strike his opponent with the first stroke from a distant interval. Like the *jodan-waza,* however, it is an advanced technique, and no explanation of it will be given here.

Oji-waza

Oji-waza is the name given to a group of techniques in which the kendoist first receives his opponent's stroke by means of slidingly pushing up, hitting down, checking, or dodging the *shinai* and then counterattacking by making use of the power of the same movement. From olden times it has been commonly said that in kendo there is no such technique as merely receiving and checking the opponent's stroke. This old saying teaches the kendoist that, once he has checked the opponent's stroke, he must by all means strike him in return. To receive the attack is to defend himself at the same time. In a kendo match, defense gives the kendoist the best chance of counterattack. If he misses such a chance, he cannot be a good kendoist.

128

93. *Men-suriage-men:* a *men* counter against a *men* attack.

Accordingly, once he defends, he must counterattack without fail. *Oji-waza* is the best technique in this case. It is a technique of innumerable variations, but according to rough classification there are four main types, which are discussed below.

1. SURIAGE-WAZA

In this technique, when the opponent is delivering a stroke, the kendoist slidingly pushes up his *shinai* just as if warding it off right upward or left upward and then delivers a stroke by taking advantage of his unbalanced posture. There are many variations in the *suriage-waza*—namely *men-suriage-men, men-suriage-do, men-suriage-kote, kote-suriage-men, kote-suriage-kote, tsuki-suriage-men,* and so forth. For beginners, two of these are most adequate—*men-suriage-men* and *kote-suriage-men*—and these are the ones discussed here.

a. *Men-suriage-men* (Fig. 93)

In case the opponent is delivering a stroke when the kendoist is in a *chudan* posture, the kendoist raises his hands while stepping backward with his left foot and pushes the opponent's *shinai* slidingly upward with the left side of his own *shinai,* so that the opponent's *shinai* is swerved aside and

129

94. *Kote-suriage-men:* a *men* counter against a *kote* attack.

his *men* left unguarded. Without a moment's delay the kendoist then delivers a *men* blow. In *suriage-waza* as a whole the timing is very important. The kendoist must snap up his wrists well so as to slightly and yet sharply push his opponent's *shinai* slidingly upward. Furthermore, he must be careful that the action of *suriage* and the swinging up of his *shinai* are not a two-step action.

b. *Kote-suriage-men* (Fig. 94)

When the opponent is delivering a stroke to the right *kote,* the kendoist steps back with his left foot first and pushes the opponent's *shinai* slidingly right oblique upward with the right side of his own *shinai,* so that the opponent's *shinai* is swerved to the right. At this moment the kendoist takes a rushing-in step and delivers a blow to his front *men.* In this case, the process of slidingly pushing up the opponent's *shinai* is nearly the same as that in *men-suriage-men.* However, the kendoist's technique should be a finer one than in *men-suriage-men,* and that is why it is essential for him to be more careful in the snapping of his wrists and the moving of his body in pushing the opponent's *shinai* slidingly upward. The same is true when the kendoist pushes up the opponent's *shinai* with the left side of his own *shinai.*

130

95. *Do-uchiotoshi-men:* a *men* counter against a *do* attack.

2. UCHIOTOSHI-WAZA

This is a technique in which the kendoist strikes his opponent's *shinai* downward with his own and strikes him by taking advantage of his un-balanced posture. The technique is not used very often, but it is most effec-tive in cases where the opponent intends to strike the kendoist's right *do*.

Do-uchiotoshi-men (Fig. 95)

When his opponent is about to strike his right *do*, the kendoist steps obliquely left backward with his left foot, strikes the opponent's *shinai* downward to the right, and strikes his front *men*. In employing this tech-nique the kendoist must be careful about the speed of the opponent's *shinai* stroke and the speed of his own striking the *shinai* downward. If these two movements do not meet well, the stroke will be unsuccessful. Therefore it is important to consider the timing well. It would be rather more effective for the kendoist to do this by twisting his right waist and snapping his wrists than by making a big *shinai* swing overhead and then bringing the *shinai* down.

131

96. *Men-nuki-do:* a *do* counter against a *men* attack.

3. KAESHI-WAZA

In this technique the kendoist receives his opponent's *shinai* with his own when the opponent swings it at him, sets it back to the other side by making use of the reflexive power given to his own *shinai,* and strikes the opponent at an unguarded point. At first glance this technique may seem to be small in stroke, but its influence is great, for the reflexive power is very strong. The kendoist must keep his palms soft and relaxed so that he can act flexibly, must consider how to move his body, and must try to make the most effective use of the opponent's strength upon striking him. Actually, the *kaeshi-waza* is a rather flashy technique which is classified into *men-kaeshi-men* (right or left *men*), *men-kaeshi-do* (right or left *do*), *kote-kaeshi-kote,* and *do-kaeshi-men.* Since all are advanced techniques, they are not explained here.

4. NUKI-WAZA

In the *nuki-waza* the kendoist lures his opponent into beating the air by dodging him and then striking him at the end of his move. To make the

132

opponent beat the air means to dodge his resolute stroke and deprive his *shinai* of its objective. Thus if the kendoist shows any sign of dodging before the opponent starts his stroke, it will be of no use. There is an old saying: "Dodge the opponent at an interval of three inches overhead." This means, in other words, "Draw the opponent near enough to you and dodge him just when he exerts himself to make a stroke, so that he cannot take any other course." In the *nuki-waza* there are the following: *men-nuki-do* (right or left *do*), *men-nuki-kote, kote-nuki-men,* and *kote-nuki-kote.* Among these those generally used and available to beginners are *men-nuki-do* (right *do*) and *kote-nuki-men.*

a. *Men-nuki-do* (Fig. 96)

When the opponent has aimed a stroke at the kendoist's *men,* the kendoist, declining his *shinai* on his left side, steps obliquely right forward as if to pass the opponent and then strikes his right *do.* The important point to remember in this case is that it is effective for the kendoist to dash in towards his opponent at the very moment when he swings his *shinai* overhead and his arms are stretched to the full. Beginners, however, are apt to keep too wide a space between themselves and the opponent. To refrain from this, the kendoist must attempt to dash into the opponent as if about to pass through him and must then twist his right waist and deliver his stroke by tightening his wrists.

b. *Kote-nuki-men*

When the opponent has directed a stroke at the kendoist's right *kote,* the kendoist first steps back with his left foot, next swings up his *shinai* to dodge the *kote* attack, and then steps straight ahead to swing his *shinai* down upon the opponent's front *men.* This is the technique of *kote-nuki-men.* Some kendoists are apt to put back their hands in an attempt to dodge the opponent's attack on their *kote,* but doing this inevitably results in being struck on the *kote.* If the kendoist swings up his *shinai* openly without fear, he will find himself unexpectedly successful.

5

Practice

Practice in kendo can be divided into two parts: basic practice and free practice, the second of which is known as *keiko*. In basic practice the kendoist, without protective armor in most cases, practices the basic and the applied techniques. Usually kendoists perform their basic practice in a group under the guidance of an instructor. In free practice the kendoists, wearing protective equipment *(bogu)*, study kendo by actually undertaking to strike one another. Free practice enables the individual kendoist to study and review his techniques while carrying them out.

Basic practice

There are two methods of basic practice: first, for the individual kendoist, without armor, to practice by himself; second, for him to practice, again without armor, with an opponent. The first of these methods can be called individual action and the second, relative action.

1. INDIVIDUAL ACTION

Kendo places great importance on practice that is carried on without an opponent. In any kind of sport, of course, proper basic techniques and forms are important. In baseball or skiing, for example, the sportsman cannot receive high marks at batting or making a turn if he is poor in basic techniques or forms. In a race or a kendo match, priority is inevitably placed upon whether the participants will win or lose, and there is no time for them to study or review their own techniques or forms in such a case.

It is therefore necessary for the kendoist to practice basic forms and techniques through individual action so that he will be able to maintain well-balanced performance in free practice as well as in matches.

If the kendoist uses protective equipment for practice from the beginning, he will naturally be affected by a temptation to practice striking his opponent or defending against his attack rather than to absorb himself in studying and reviewing his own techniques and forms. Accordingly, the first thing the kendoist must do is to practice the proper basic actions and strokes through individual action in order to build up steady techniques and well-balanced forms, thus preparing for bouts and matches in the future. Moreover, the kendoist can practice through individual action as much as he likes, if only he is determined to try.

2. RELATIVE ACTION

Once the kendoist has done a good job of learning the basic techniques and forms, he may undertake the next step: relative action or practice with an opponent. There are three types of relative action: practice between two students, practice with a knocking stick or a knocking base, and practice between an instructor and a student.

a. Practice between students

The relative action of students versus students is a method in which students, facing each other at a fixed interval, mutually practice the basic strokes and the applied techniques again and again. This differs from individual action in that the student on one side need not merely beat the air but may practice the proper way to hit the student on the other side. At the same time, the student on the other side should be so prepared that his opponent can practice easily.

As a rule, the method of students versus students is one by which students practice collectively under the guidance of their instructor, and satisfactory results are achieved in a short time. This being the case, it is not a method for pure beginners in kendo, nor is it sufficient to teach more advanced students the precise and delicate points of kendo art.

b. Practice with a knocking stick or a knocking base

Until the kendoist really practices hitting objects, he cannot understand by himself how to tighten his hands and arms and how to keep a well-balanced posture, no matter what splendid forms and techniques he may have learned. Therefore it is necessary for him to fully practice these forms and techniques with the knocking stick and the knocking base prior to putting on armor and exchanging strokes with his opponent. He can make a knocking stick or a knocking base for himself, and it is advisable for him to set them up in the yard or somewhere in the house so that he can practice with them.

c. Practice of instructor versus student

In kendo an individual is matched against an individual. The kendoist may strike his opponent freely, but at the same time he may deliver a stroke if only he can catch the kendoist in an unguarded moment. Moreover, the opponent does not stand still. In other words, a match is much different from hitting such stable objects as a knocking stick or a knocking post. Naturally, the technique of learning how to seize a chance of striking the opponent must be regarded as an important factor in kendo training. Practice with an instructor fundamentally teaches these points. The instructor makes various prior agreements with the student regarding which points to strike, so that the student may strike these points whenever the instructor assumes a fixed posture inviting the strike.

Free practice

Free practice is called either *keiko* or *jiyu-renshu*. As to the terminology, it is not so long since the word *keiko* began to be used in the sense of *renshu* or practice. Its original meaning, however, was to meditate upon and study the exemplary things of olden times. In time, its meaning came to be that of training or cultivation.

In kendo it is required that the kendoist strike or thrust at his objective instantly and very accurately. If an action is undertaken only after deliberating about it, it is too late. Once the kendoist has made a decision to initiate an action, he must put it into effect without a moment's delay. In other words, all his actions must be made reflexively with lightning speed. Such reflexive action can never be mastered by being practiced only once or twice or for any brief space of time. The kendoist cannot perform it until

137

he has practiced it over and over again. It was probably from this point of view that the word *keiko* was changed from its earlier meaning of training or cultivating to imply practice.

It is to be hoped that the kendoist will consider the significance of this and that he will never give up practicing until he becomes a truly good kendoist. He may think that if he only learns kendo he will soon become a great kendoist or a master swordsman. But, as the proverb says, Rome was not built in a day, and no kendoist can succeed without perpetual effort.

1. METHODS OF PRACTICE

There are three methods of free practice in kendo: *kakari-geiko* or attack practice, *gokaku-geiko* or equal practice, and *hikitate-geiko* or assistance practice. (The "k" of *keiko* becomes "g" in the combined form.) Beginners are thoroughly trained in *kakari-geiko* so that they will grasp the fundamental techniques of kendo. Once they have acquired these fundamental techniques, they mutually practice the more delicate and refined techniques and proceed to the mental aspects of kendo. Then, when they are good at these things, they proceed to the other forms of *keiko*.

a. *Kakari-geiko*

In this method, beginners practice with their seniors. It is not very effective for a junior kendoist to engage in *gokaku-geiko* with a senior, but for him to perform his *waza* and actively attack the senior is effective in cultivating his body and improving his *waza*.

Once the beginning kendoist faces his opponent, he feels as though the interval between himself and the opponent were greater than it actually is, even though he is very good at the basic techniques he has learned through practice by himself. The opponent's *shinai* also disturbs him, so that he cannot easily strike the opponent as he would like to do. As he repeats his practice again and again, however, he naturally learns how to attack his opponent effectively.

Moreover, the kendoist must not be hasty in his attempt to strike his opponent. If he continues to make inaccurate strokes or permits himself improper posture during his practice, the practice will not be effective in spite of his efforts. On the contrary, he will acquire bad habits and will find it difficult to amend them in the future. In a word, beginners must not be hasty but must endeavor to practice steady strokes one by one in a proper posture.

One more thing the beginner must be careful about in *kakari-geiko* is the footwork. If there is any inaccuracy in his strokes, the reason will be that he is inclined to move his *shinai* with his arms only and that the strokes are not accompanied by good footwork. In fact, it is advisable for the kendoist, when attacking, to work his feet and legs rather than his arms and hands.

b. *Gokaku-geiko*

Gokaku-geiko is practice between two kendoists of equal or similar ability carried out in the atmosphere of a real match. In such instances, the kendoists decide the winner and the loser by themselves. For this reason it is also called a self-judging match. If one of the kendoists is struck and calls out *"Maitta"* (I'm beaten), it means that the other gains the point. If the two are not conscientious, however, practice of this kind will not be properly performed.

In *kakari-geiko,* as mentioned above, the kendoist does nothing but attack actively and continuously—a good way for him to train in basic matters such as method of strokes, posture, guard, and footwork. This however, is not enough for his kendo training. Kendo's most delicate factors—the interval between opponents, the chances of attack, and the tricks employed in attack and defense—will not be learned until the kendoist begins *gokaku-geiko*. This form of practice, accordingly, is the most important matter in kendo—the means by which the kendoist acquires his techniques, trains his mind, and improves his kendo art.

c. *Hikitate-geiko*

This method of practice is the opposite of *kakari-geiko*. It is a method in which a senior guides a junior while fighting. *Hikitate-geiko* is undertaken when the kendoist's ability in the art has already been comparatively well improved through *kakari-geiko* and *gokaku-geiko*. This may be of little concern to beginning kendoists, but it will be useful in the future when they have become good at kendo and have an opportunity to instruct their

139

juniors in *kakari-geiko*. Through *kakari-geiko,* however, some beginners will improve and others will not, depending on the method of guidance employed by the senior kendoist in the practice.

The proper way to guide beginners is as follows. If the beginner attacks the senior in a proper way, the senior must intentionally take such an attitude and posture that the junior can naturally and easily strike to the point. On the other hand, in case the beginner attacks in an improper way, the senior must dodge, check, or suppress that attack so that the junior can naturally discover that his stroke was delivered incorrectly. If the senior simply suppressed or checked the beginner's strokes, on the contrary, the beginner would not improve his techniques but would become depressed and might lose interest in kendo. In any event, the important point of *hikitate-geiko* is to create conditions in which beginners can practice kendo cheerfully and positively.

2. VARIOUS PROBLEMS IN PRACTICE

In undertaking *keiko* the kendoist is wrong if he thinks that he can improve his techniques only by attacking his opponent ardently. There are many other things of which he must be careful in practicing kendo. The following are a few points that are regarded as especially important.

a. The *metsuke*

The *metsuke* means the point of observation: the point aimed at when one kendoist is facing another. This is as important as the footwork. In kendo it is first of all important to observe the opponent. Still, the kendoist cannot take so much time in observing the opponent as he does in watching a movie or seeing a painting or a sculpture. He is required to observe in a moment and to judge instantly. In this sense, the *metsuke* is most important.

From olden times it has been said that the eye must be poured into the opponent's eyes, the point of his sword, or his fists. The most basic of these is the opponent's eyes. There is a common saying that the eye represents the mind: if the opponent thinks anything in his mind, it is reflected in his eyes. If the kendoist watches his opponent's eyes only, however, he cannot observe his whole movement. The best way to see the opponent is to look at his whole body while paying particular attention to his eyes, to the point of his sword, and to his fists. The kendoist will be able to do this by watching his opponent with a mind like that of looking toward a mountain far away. This is called *enzan no metsuke:* the distant-mountain point of observation.

What is of further importance regarding the *metsuke* is the "two eye-sights" *(kanken),* as spoken of by Musashi Miyamoto in his book on swordsmanship, *Gorin no Sho.* Musashi pointed out that *kan* (seeing through or into) should be done strongly and *ken* (looking) weakly. The substantial meaning is this: when looking at his opponent, the kendoist must be keen in seeing through his mind but mild in observing his superficial appearance. Superficial appearance in this case means the opponent's physical build, the armor he wears, and his technical abilities.

If the opponent is physically strong or wears a splendid set of armor, the kendoist is apt to think of him as a really strong fencer. But to have an inferiority complex in the presence of his opponent means that the kendoist has already been beaten mentally before the contest begins. If only the kendoist sees properly into his opponent's mind, he will find that he is not such a formidable fencer as he seemed at first glance. This is an important point for the kendoist to study. If he is well prepared, he will not be agitated by anybody, no matter how strong he may appear at first.

b. The yells

At a kendo match or during practice the fencers yell *"Yaa!"* or *"Oh!"* upon facing each other in a fixed posture or *"Men!"*, *"Kote!"*, *"Do!"*, or *"Tsuki!"* when they advance for strokes. The yells are for the following purposes. First of all, by yelling, the kendoist's spirit and body are concentrated on one point, enabling him to put forth a strong fighting spirit against his opponent. Second, he can make sure of his action or his stroke in case of attack and show his strong confidence that he will never be affected by anybody or anything. To yell or to shout also expresses a natural need to exert the strength that he has in his body.

For this reason, beginners must shout aloud at the start of a match or practice and launch a positive fight by putting forth everything they have in them. When yelling, however, beginners are apt to use their throats only. The beginning kendoist must try to raise his shout from his lower belly—that is, by settling his strength around his lower belly. A superficial yell from the throat only does not enable him to have a full fighting spirit or increase his self-confidence.

c. The interval: *maai*

The *maai* means the interval or space between the two fencers, and it is a very important matter in kendo. Although it may be a little too difficult for beginners to learn, clear understanding of the *maai* has a definite influence on the outcome of a match, and it is advisable for beginners to study it. The three types of *maai* are described below.

(1) *Issoku-itto no ma* (interval for a stroke at a step forward): In the *issoku-itto no ma* (also called *uchima* or stroke interval) the points of the two kendoists' *shinai* are crossed about one inch from the tip. At this interval, if the kendoist takes a step forward, he can strike his opponent. In delivering a stroke, the kendoist must be at this interval without fail. It is the one used oftenest in kendo matches and practice, and it is essential for beginners to study it well.

(2) *To-ma* (distant interval): This is a larger interval than the *issoku-itto no ma* and is rather often used at kendo matches. During the time that the two kendoists are drawing toward each other from the *to-ma* to the *issoku-itto no ma* they may exchange various tactics, such as the sword-point check, which is very important in kendo. This is somewhat too difficult for beginners to understand, but as they improve in the art of kendo they find it very important to master this interval.

(3) *Chika-ma* (near interval) This is a nearer interval than the *issoku-itto no ma*. At this interval the kendoist can strike his opponent without stepping forward, but he must naturally be cautious, since his opponent has the same advantage. Once the kendoist finds himself at this interval, he must seize the opportunity for attack. If he cannot do this, he must approach nearer so that he and his opponent will be pushing each other's *shinai* guard *(tsuba-zeriai)*. Otherwise he must step back and place himself at a greater interval. In either case, he must continue to hold his opponent's *shinai* with his own to avoid being counterattacked by the opponent.

d. The working of the sword point *(kissaki)*: When the kendoist faces his opponent in the *chudan* posture, he must always be attacking him with the point of his *shinai*. In other words the *kissaki* (sword point) must always be aiming at the center (key point) of the opponent. The two kendoists are

142

eager to control each other's center, and here occurs a struggle for that center. The working of the *kissaki* is divided into four elements: to touch, to press, to let spring back, and to ward off the opponent's *shinai*. At a real match or during practice the kendoist can give his opponent a stroke after controlling the point of his *shinai* by employing this working of the *kissaki*. If, however, the kendoist attacks him without paying attention to the point of his *shinai,* he will not be able to give him an effective stroke. On the contrary, he may receive a stroke from the opponent. Beginners are likely to be careless about this, but it is essential that they study it to the best of their ability.

e. The three ways of attack. There are various tactics in kendo practice and matches, but three basic tactics stand out. The first of these is to attack the opponent's *shinai:* the second, to attack his technique *(waza);* the third, to attack his spirit. To attack the opponent's *shinai* is to manage to control his *kissaki* so that it will not control the kendoist's center, as explained above. To attack the opponent's *waza* is to try using the *waza* he is good at before he is able to use it or to attack the weak point underlying his favorite *waza*. If the kendoist tries his opponent's favorite *waza* before he himself can use it, his opponent is forestalled and cannot employ that *waza*. A favorite technique has its strong points, of course, but it also has its weak ones. If the kendoist attacks his opponent at that weak point, he is prevented from using his favorite technique. To attack the opponent's spirit is to attack him suddenly with more vital yells than his. In this case, the opponent is so surprised and depressed at the kendoist's shouts that he cannot make a positive attack. The beginning kendoist will discover a great variety of tactics in matches and practice and it is advisable for him to study all of them.

f. The three good chances of attack: When the kendoist wishes to give his opponent a stroke, it will not be successful for him to attack at random. It is, after all, important to seize a good opportunity for attack. There are three good chances: at the moment when the opponent is about to start his motion, when he has just finished his motion, and when he is settled. Any action has its beginning, and the moment when the opponent's action is about to start gives the kendoist the best chance of attack. If he attacks the opponent at this moment, the opponent cannot ward off the stroke.

143

From the scientific point of view there are various complicated reasons for this. Briefly speaking, however, the reason is as follows. Just before one starts a motion, one's strength is concentrated. If the motion is really started, it will be powerful. But at the moment when it is about to start, one is at a standstill. Kendoists who are able to give a stroke without missing this moment are considered to be men of clear insight and excellent kendo artists.

The second good chance for attack comes when an action of the opponent has just ended. At this moment his body and his mind are both too much stretched to dodge the kendoist's attack. The moment when the opponent is settled (the third good chance for attack) resembles the moment when he has just completed an action, but it is a little different in its quality. It is the moment when his action has fallen to a standstill both mentally and physically, and it comes in the course of his successive actions as he pauses for breath. It is a critical moment for both the kendoist and his opponent, and it deserves the most careful attention.

Glossary

(Although long vowels in Japanese words are not indicated in the text, they are marked here for the guidance of the reader.)

ageru	上げる	to raise, lift up, hold up
aite	相　手	opponent, partner (in a bout or match)
aiuchi	相　打	tie, draw, simultaneous scoring of points by both kendoists
arigatō	ありがとう	thank you
ashi	足	leg, foot
ashi no ura	足 の 裏	sole of the foot
ashi no yubi	足 の 指	toes
atama	頭	head, top, top of the head
atatamaru	暖まる	to get warm, to warm oneself through exercise
ateru	当てる	to hit, strike, score a point, knock against
ato-uchi	あと打ち	delayed blow (almost like a feint in boxing), jab
au	会　う	to meet, encounter an opponent
bōgu	防　具	kendo armor
banzai	万　歳	hurrah, cheer (after a contest)
bokken	木　剣	wooden sword used as practice weapon
bokutō	木　刀	same as *bokken*
budō	武　道	chivalry, way of knighthood (old historical term)
bushi	武　士	samurai, knight

145

Glossary

Bushidō	武 士 道	the way of the samurai
chikai	近 い	close, near, face to face (with an opponent)
chika-ma	近 間	near interval
chikara	力	strength, power
chūdan no kamae	中段の構え	position of the *shinai* at the ready—with point aimed at center of opponent just above belt line
daisensei	大 先 生	polite word for a teacher who holds tenth rank in kendo (literally "great teacher")
dan	段	rank, grade
dantai	団 体	group, members of a group
debana-waza	出 端 業	attacking-at-the-start technique
dasu	出 す	put forward, extend (foot, hand, etc.)
dō	胴	trunk, waist, chest armor, the *dō* point or strike
dōgu	道 具	equipment, entire kendo equipment (generally equipment tied together and placed in a bag)
dōjō	道 場	fencing hall
fumu	踏 む	to step, take a step, move (in any direction)
furu	振 る	to swing, raise and lower (the *shinai*)
futari	二 人	two persons, two opponents meeting for a match
futatsu	二 つ	two things, two
gakkō	学 校	school
gedan no kamae	下段の構え	position of the *shinai* when held lower than waist with point towards the floor
godan	五 段	fifth rank in kendo
gōkaku-geiko	互格稽古	practice between kendoists of equal ability

146

gomen	御　免	pardon me, excuse me (generally used when leaving the fencing hall)
hachidan	八　段	eighth rank in kendo
hachimaki	鉢　巻	towel used as headband under *men*
hai	は　い	yes, acknowledgment
hajime	始　め	begin (command at start of match)
hakama	袴	divided skirt, skirtlike trousers
hanshi	範　士	outstanding fencer of eighth to tenth rank
hansoku	反　則	violation of a (kendo) rule, misconduct
hantai	反　対	opposite
hantei	判　定	judgment, decision
hara	腹	abdomen, stomach area
harai-waza	払い業	warding-off technique
harau	払　う	to parry by brushing away the opponent's *shinai*
hashi	端	boundary line of match area
hashiru	走　る	to run
hassō no kamae	八相の構え	position of the *shinai* held vertically (with both hands) at right side of head and at shoulder level
hata	旗	referee's flag
hidari	左	left, left side
hidari-dō	左　胴	a blow on the left side of the *dō*
hidari-jōdan-men	左上段面	a blow on the left side of the *men*
hidari-kote	左 小 手	a blow on the left *kote*
hidari-men	左　面	a blow on the left side of the *men*
hiji	肘	elbow
hikitate-geiko	引立稽古	practice in which a senior guides a junior
hikiwake	引　分	a draw in a kendo match (generally a time lapse without either kendoist's scoring)

147

Glossary

hiki-waza	引 業	stepping-back technique
hikui	低 い	low (i.e., the blow struck was too low)
himo	紐	string, cord, strings used in tying on kendo armor
iai	居 合	sword exercise embodying a series of cutting and thrusting movements in drawing and returning the blade
ichi	一	the number one
iie	い い え	no
ippon	一 本	one point, single blow, one-point match
issoku-ittō no ma	一足一刀の間	interval for a stroke at a step forward
jiyū	自 由	freedom (of movement, etc.)
jiyū-renshū	自由練習	free practice
jōdan no kamae	上段の構え	position of the *shinai* held above the head with one or both hands or held in front with the right or the left hand
jōdan-waza	上 段 業	technique of holding the *shinai* over the head
jūdan	十 段	tenth or highest rank in kendo
kachinuki	勝 抜 き	match in which a kendoist meets all opponents in succession until he is defeated, after which the winner continues in the same fashion, decision going to kendoist who has scored most wins
kaeshi-waza	返 業	technique of receiving opponent's stroke and deflecting it with the reflexive power of the *shinai*
kakari-geiko	掛り稽古	attack practice
kakegoe	掛 声	shout, yell
kamae	構	basic kendo positions, guard positions
kangeiko	寒 稽 古	winter practice
kankyaku	観 客	spectators at a kendo match

148

kata	形	old-style form of kendo employing steel blades; exercises
katana	刀	sword, long sword
katate-waza	片手業	single-hand techniques
katsu	勝つ	to win
katsugi-waza	担業	shouldering-the-sword technique to make a swift dodge or sidestep movement to avoid being attacked
keiko	稽古	practice
keikogi	稽古着	kendoist's jacket
keirei	敬礼	formal salute or bow made very slowly from the waist
kendō	剣道	kendo, Japanese fencing
kissaki	剣先	point of sword or *shinai*
kiai	気合	shout of self-encouragement or self-assertion
kirikaeshi	切返し	warming-up exercise with the *shinai*
kote	小手	hand armor, protective mitt, the *kote* point
kudan	九段	ninth rank in kendo
kyōshi	教士	degree or title for fencers of sixth or seventh rank
maai	間合	distance between two kendoists
mae	前	front, forward
makeru	負ける	to be defeated, lose
mamoru	守る	to defend, protect
mannaka	真中	center, exact center
masshōmen	真正面	directly in front
mate	待て	wait, hold up a minute
matsu	待つ	to wait
mawaru	廻る	to turn around
me	目	eye
men	面	mask, face guard, the *men* point
metsuke	目付	point of observation

Glossary

migi	右	right, right side
migi-dō	右 胴	a blow on the right side of the *do*
migi-kote	右 小 手	a blow on the right *kote*
migi-men	右 面	a blow on the right side of the *men*
mune	胸	chest
nagai	長 い	long (in length)
naka	中	inside
nidan	二 段	second rank in kendo
nidan-waza	二 段 業	two-step technique
nuki-waza	抜 業	technique of luring opponent to make a stroke and then dodging it
nuku	抜 く	to draw the *shinai* or sword
ōji-waza	応 じ 業	defense-plus-counterattack technique
ōkii	大 き い	big, large
osu	押 す	to push, shove (the opponent—generally a foul in kendo)
rei	礼	bow, command to bow
renshi	錬 士	fencer of the fourth to sixth rank
renshū	練 習	practice, training period
rokudan	六 段	sixth rank in kendo
sagaru	下 が る	to retreat, back up
sageru	下 げ る	to lower (the point of the *shinai*)
sakigawa	先 革	leather tip of the shinai
sandan	三 段	third rank in kendo
sandan-waza	三 段 業	three-step technique
sasu	差 す	to thrust a sword or a *shinai* forward; to wear a sword by thrusting it through the obi
shiai	試 合	match, contest
shiaijō	試 合 場	contest area
shichidan	七 段	seventh rank in kendo
shikake-waza	仕 掛 業	technique of delivering a stroke by taking advantage of opponent's being off guard
shimpan	審 判	referee

150

shinai	竹 刀	fencing stave used in kendo
shizentai	自 然 体	natural standing position
shodan	初 段	first rank in kendo
shōmen	正 面	front view
shoshinsha	初 心 者	beginner in kendo
sode	袖	sleeve
sonkyo	蹲 踞	crouch position
soto	外	outside, outer area
suburi	素 振 り	exercise in movement of *shinai* to simulate striking of points
suriage-waza	摺上げ業	technique of warding off opponent's *shinai* with sliding, upward movement and then delivering stroke by taking advantage of his unbalanced posture
suwaru	座 る	to sit down
tachi	太 刀	long sword
tai-atari	体 当 り	body contact
tai-iku	体 育	physical education
taijū	体 重	body weight
taikai	大 会	tournament
take	竹	bamboo
tare	垂	kendo waist armor
tatsu	立 つ	to stand (in position)
te	手	hand
temoto	手 元	grip
tō-ma	遠 間	distant interval
tsuba	鍔	guard on *shinai* or sword
tsuka	柄	leather cover on handle of *shinai*
tsuki	突 き	throat flap of *men*, thrust to the throat
uchima	打 間	same as *issoku-ittō no ma*
uchiotoshi-waza	打落し業	technique of striking opponent's *shinai* downward and taking advantage of his unbalanced posture
ude	腕	arm
ue	上	upper part, above

151

Glossary

ukeru	受ける	to block a blow
ukedachi	受太刀	defensive position, counterattack
ura	裏	reverse, reverse side
ushiro	後	back, behind
utsu	打つ	to strike, hit
wakeru	分ける	to part or separate two kendoists
wakigamae	脇構	method of holding the *shinai* horizontal and extended at either side of the body
waza	技	technique, form in delivering blows
yame	止め	halt, stop (command to end a bout or a match)
yasumu	休む	to rest, halt for a rest
yodan	四段	fourth rank in kendo
yokomen	横面	a blow to the side of the head just above the ear
yoroshii	宜しい	good, very nice
yoru	寄る	to approach, come closer
yubi	指	finger
Zen-Beikoku Kendō Remmei	全米国剣道連盟	All-American Kendo Federation
Zen-Nippon Gakusei Kendō Remmei	全日本学生剣道連盟	All-Japan Student Kendo Federation
Zen-Nippon Kendō Remmei	全日本剣道連盟	All-Japan Kendo Federation

Bibliography

(*Books in Japanese are indicated by parenthetical translations of their titles.*)

Gakko Kendo Kenkyukai (Society for the Study of School Kendo): *Gakko Kendo no Shido* (Guide for Teaching Kendo in School), Shubunsha, Tokyo, 1958

Hiyashi, Sansei: *Kendo Hoten* (Dictionary of Kendo), Mizuhosha, Tokyo, 1953

Inami, Hakusui: *Nippon To* (The Japanese Sword), Cosmo Publishing Co., Tokyo 1948

Kaneko, Kinji: *Kendo Gaku* (Learning Kendo), Shibundo Shoten, Tokyo, 1929

Kashiwai, S.: *Kendo no Manabikata* (Styles in Learning Kendo), Kinensha, Tokyo, 1956

Mitamura, Kunihiko: *Dai Nippon Naginata Kyohan* (The Study of Japanese Naginata), Shubundo Shoten, Tokyo, 1938

Nagai, Takaichiro; Otaki, Tado; and Nakano, Yasoji: *Sumo, Judo, Kendo* (Sumo, Judo, and Kendo), Popurasha, Tokyo, 1960

Nakayama, Hiromichi: *Nippon Kendo to Seiyo Kengi* (Japanese Kendo and Western Sword Techniques), Shimbi Shoin, Tokyo, 1937

Nawata, Tadao: *Kendo no Riron to Jissai* (The Theory and Practice of Kendo), Rokumeikan, Tokyo, 1938

Nitobe, Inazo: *Bushido: The Soul of Japan,* G. P. Putnam's Sons, New York, 1905

Noma, Hisashi: *Kendo Tokuhon* (Textbook of Kendo), Dai Nippon Yubenkai Kodansha, Tokyo, 1939

Noma, Seiji: *Budo Hokan* (Handbook of Martial Arts), Dai Nippon Yubenkai Kodansha, Tokyo, 1934

Numata, Yorisuke: *Nippon Monshogaku* (Study of Japanese Crests), Meiji Shoin, Tokyo, 1926

Sasamori, Junzo: *Kendo* (Kendo), Obunsha, Tokyo, 1955

Shimizu, Mura: *Token Zensho* (Study of the Sword), Seikokan, Tokyo, 1926

Shimogawa, C.: *Kendo no Hattatsu* (The Progress of Kendo), Dai Nippon Butoku-kai Hombu, Kyoto, 1925

153

Bibliography

Takano, Hiromasa: *Shin Kendo* (The New Kendo), Meishinsha, Tokyo, 1933

Uragami, Eietsu, and Takeuchi, J.: *Kyudo* (Archery), Kembunsha, Tokyo, 1928

Warner, Gordon: "An Old Sword Flashes in the Dark Shadow," *Black Belt Magazine,* Vol. I, No. 3, Los Angeles, April 1962

——: "Bushido: Misused and Misunderstood," *Kashu Mainichi,* Los Angeles, December 1959

——: "Swords and Armor of Europe and Japan," *Black Belt Magazine,* Vol. I, No. 2, Los Angeles, January 1962

——: "Tiger in the Forest," *Rafu Shimpo,* Los Angeles, January 1961

Wataya, Setsu: *Nippon Bugei Shoden* (History of Japanese Martial Arts), Jimbutsu Oraisha, Tokyo, 1961

Yamada, A.; Ito, C.; and Motoori, S.: *Bujutsu Sosho* (The Martial Arts), Hiroya Kokusho Kankokai, Tokyo, 1925

Yamada, Jirokichi: *Nippon Kendo Shi* (History of Japanese Kendo), Suishinsha, Tokyo, 1922

——: *Shinshin Shuyo to Kendo Shugi* (Physical and Mental Training in Kendo), 2 vols., Suishinsha, Tokyo, 1923

Yumoto, John M.: *The Samurai Sword: A Handbook,* Charles E. Tuttle Co., Inc., Rutland, Vermont, and Tokyo

Index

155

Index

156

Index

158